LAWYERS

AND

WELL-BEING

Title: Lawyers and Well-Being / Fernando Messias

Author: Fernando Messias

ISBN 978-93-6354-691-2

Cyberwit.net

HIG 45 Kaushambi Kunj, Kalindipuram

Allahabad - 211011 (U.P.) India

W. http://www.cyberwit.net / E. info@cyberwit.net

T. + (91) 9415091004 + (91) (532) 2552257

Printed at Repro India Limited.

Table of contents

Foreword by lawyer, Dr Raquel Sampaio, Executive Director of the Mental Law Association ("Associação Direito Mental")

The publication of this book is a significant contribution to academic and applied reflection on the intersection between the practice of law and the promotion of well-being, at a time when mental health in the legal profession is, more than ever, an unavoidable priority. Throughout my career as a lawyer and as founder and director of the Mental Law Association, I have repeatedly witnessed the harmful effects of a legal culture that often normalises exhaustion and neglects well-being. It was precisely the urgency of transforming this reality that led us, in 2023, in partnership with ProChild CoLAB and the Psychology Research Centre at the University of Minho, to develop the study 'The impact of organisational culture on the mental health and well-being of legal professionals'. This survey, a pioneer in Portugal, made it possible to document, based on data from more than 800 participants, clinically significant levels of depression, anxiety and burnout symptoms among legal professionals, with a special incidence among women and younger professionals. It is in this context that this book takes on added relevance. Through a dialogue between the foundations of Positive Psychology, contemporary leadership models and the specificities of the practice of law, the author offers a valuable contribution to understanding and transforming the daily professional lives of lawyers. His proposal for leadership that promotes well-being is not only theoretically sound - it is also ethically necessary. This is a book that complements and reinforces the work of Mental Law Association: raising the profile of pressing issues, increasing mental health literacy, and building more humane, sustainable and just legal structures. We believe that the transformation of law starts here - with the care of those who do it every day.

I congratulate the author, Dr Fernando Messias, for the courage, rigour and depth with which he has approached this subject. His research makes an indispensable contribution not only to the academic debate, but also to the transformative practice of the legal professions.

Raquel Sampaio

(Lawyer, Executive Director of the Mental Law Association)

Foreword by Dr Saúl Neves de Jesus, Professor of Psychology

It is often said that 'there are no two without three' ...

Having already written the Foreword to two of Fernando Messias' previous books, I was delighted to be invited to preface this one. Each of the books has very distinct characteristics, revealing the multiplicity of contributions that Fernando has made in his career and the excellence he has shown in different fields. In the first book, entitled 'Heterónimos', he revealed his literary ability, creating various stories about characters with their own identity, expressing his imagination, almost stepping outside of himself and entering into the 'I' of each character. In particular, the character Edmund

Stolkin, who himself became the author of Fernando's last published book, "The King and the Queen. The Arehns family", last year (2024).

In turn, in the second book, entitled "Colour and the word. Creativity and subjectivity of styles in visual art", he presents us with images of some of his artistic works, accompanied by his reflections on these works produced over the years, almost summarising and taking stock of his own journey in the visual arts.

The creativity that Fernando Messias has shown in both written and visual art is really quite remarkable, demonstrating his ability to write with light and words.

After revealing himself in the written and visual arts, he now presents us with a book with more technical characteristics and a scientific basis, bridging the gap between his legal training and that which he also pursued in psychology.

'LAWYERS AND WELL-BEING' is a contribution to understanding well-being and mental health in the legal profession, without forgetting the individual that each person is.

As the Introduction begins, 'This book deals with the impact of the legal profession on the well-being of lawyers', considering that physical-psychic-emotional balance is essential for the effective exercise of this demanding profession. After all, lawyers seek to contribute to the well-being of their clients. But who contributes to their own well-being? It explains that high levels of well-being can contribute to better professional performance and quality of service for clients, but that the legal profession is facing a mental health crisis, with lawyers experiencing high levels of depression, anxiety and addiction compared to other professions, and that it is essential to adopt organisational practices and create legislative changes that contribute to improving working conditions and preserving the well-being of legal professionals, i.e. measures that allow lawyers to obtain greater support and protection in situations where their mental health and well-being are unbalanced.

In terms of structure, the book begins with an Introduction, followed by Chapter I, 'The Lawyer, Well-being and Positive Psychology', which analyses, among other topics, concepts and theories of well-being, the importance of positive behaviour in individuals and organisations and leadership that promotes well-being. Chapter II presents 'Studies into the Health and Well-being of Lawyers'. The book ends with some 'Conclusions and recommendations'. Of particular interest is the approach to leadership as a promoter of well-being, but considering lawyers as leaders of themselves, someone who should also seek to build a path based on healthy lifestyles, as emphasised in the study 'Life in the Law 2020/21', as well as in the work carried out by the Mental Law Association in Portugal.

With a focus on Positive Psychology, the perspective should be above all preventative, rather than just remedial, so that everyone can optimise their potential, contributing to their own well-being and professional success.

In this way, Fernando Messias integrates his professional learning with the learning he has acquired during his training, particularly in the field of psychology, a scientific area in which he did a post-doctorate, completed in 2022, which I had the opportunity to supervise.

I hope that Fernando continues to present us with more literary, artistic and scientific works, somewhat in the vein of his heteronym Edmund Stolkin, who lived 103 years with quality of life and well-being throughout his career...

Saul Neves de Jesus

(Professor of Psychology at the University of the Algarve)

Acknowledgements

I would like to express my gratitude to all those who made themselves available and supported this work.

I would like to express my deepest gratitude to LawCare, a British organisation dedicated to promoting mental health in the legal community, whose availability allowed me to deepen my understanding of the cross-cutting nature of this issue in international legal communities.

My sincere thanks also go to Associação Direito Mental, a Portuguese organisation that promotes a positive culture of support for mental health in the legal community, in particular its director, Dr Raquel Sampaio, for her essential collaboration in the development of this work.

I would like to thank Dr João Quintas, president of the Institute of Young Portuguese Lawyers, for facilitating contact with the Mental Law Association and for his availability throughout this project.

I also acknowledge the role of the British organisations Law Society and Solicitors Regulation Authority in facilitating contact with LawCare, as well as the International Bar Association (IBA) - the largest global organisation of legal professionals - for the work of the Presidential Task Force on Mental Well-being in the Legal Profession, developed in collaboration with the Legal Policy & Research Unit. This co-operation culminated in the report 'Mental Well-being in the

Legal Profession: A Global Study', which establishes fundamental principles for promoting the mental health of lawyers at an international level.

Finally, special thanks to the preface writers who kindly contributed introductory texts, without which this work would be incomplete.

(My) life is like being hit with it.

Book of Disquiet by Bernardo Soares

Vol. II. Fernando Pessoa

Introduction

This book addresses the impact of the legal profession on lawyers' well-being.

The relationship between the legal profession and well-being, which forms the basis of this book, is conceptualised here as the physical, psychological and emotional balance of the individual in relation to their profession.

In concrete terms, the completion of a law degree and subsequent enrolment in the Bar Association marks the beginning of an ethical and professional journey - commonly known as a 'career' - through which the professional asserts themselves in society as an active member of the legal profession, with the aim of exercising their activity competently and effectively.

In this socio-professional context, lawyers interact simultaneously in multiple spheres: professional, family, personal and social. In this complex dynamic, psychophysical balance is both a constant and a decisive variable in professional performance. Self-control takes centre stage here: the quality of professional practice correlates directly with the lawyer's degree of internal balance, and is a positive leadership factor.

This establishes the premise of well-being - in its objective, subjective, emotional and psychological dimensions. It should be emphasised that the effective practice of a demanding profession such as law is unfeasible without this fundamental condition of balance.

The lawyer, from an essential perspective, is the professional who practises law - the activity of providing legal assistance through procedural leadership with the aim of achieving justice. This requires the completion of academic training, a supervised professional internship, passing the Bar exams and practical experience in legal proceedings. These stages enable you to exercise technical legal functions, including representation in court and the strict fulfilment of judicial mandates.

The notion of 'being a lawyer' also encompasses the dimensions of patron and legal protector, implying skills of defence, sponsorship and legal representation. The Constitution of the Portuguese Republic enshrines this activity as an essential state function (Articles 9 and 20), and it is the state's responsibility to guarantee not only access to justice and legal advice, but also the right to legal representation before any entity. This dual condition - both a social role and a professional status - configures a relationship of influence and subjection analogous to the processes of emerging leadership.

Lawyers - male or female - are therefore required to have technical competence combined with permanent psychophysical stability. Well-being and mental health are paramount requirements, although practical reality often distances itself from this socio-professional ideal.

The contemporary context places increasing demands on efficiency, technical mastery, resistance to pressure and the ability to meet tight deadlines. This situation requires legal professionals to have high levels of resilience, continuous academic preparation and the ability to manage multidimensional personal and professional challenges.

It is now recognised that the legal profession is facing a mental health crisis, with lawyers experiencing high levels of depression, anxiety and addiction compared to other professions.

It's a fact - society demands it and legal professionals take on the responsibility of defending their constituents and, in this dynamic, anxiety and sometimes imbalance (more or less accentuated) arise.

This reality alerts us to the need to promote interventions in terms of mental health and well-being, as well as resilience in the legal community. This is a relevant topic, for at least five reasons that immediately spring to mind.

The first relates to mental health: lawyers' well-being is directly linked to their mental health. Dealing with high levels of stress, work pressure and exposure to emotionally challenging situations can have a negative impact on the mental health of legal professionals. Promoting well-being contributes positively to preventing anxiety, depression and burnout.

Another reason has to do with professional performance: legal professionals who are physically and mentally well tend to be more productive, creative and efficient at work. High levels of well-being can contribute to better professional performance and quality of service to clients.

A third reason could be talent retention: encouraging the well-being of legal professionals can help retain talent in the legal profession. Legal professionals who feel supported and cared for are more likely to stay in the workplace and make a significant contribution to their organisations.

A fourth reason, I would say, could be the image of the profession itself: concern for the well-being of legal professionals also influences the image of the profession in society. Promoting care for the mental health and well-being of legal professionals can improve the profession's reputation and attract younger people to the profession.

Lastly, I would say cost savings: investing in well-being programmes can result in long-term benefits, such as reduced absenteeism, increased productivity and lower costs related to mental health problems, benefiting both legal professionals and organisations. Just to start with a few reasons why I'm interested in this topic. Given this reality, I would say that the answer to 'the impact of the legal profession on lawyers' well-being' can be found, in part, in psychology.

Positive Psychology has a vast field of application in this area, as will be discussed below, proposing concrete support mechanisms for legal professionals. This book analyses the contemporary challenges facing the legal profession and the potential of this psychological approach as a professional support tool.

The structure of the book is divided into two core

chapters, corresponding to the themes of 'Lawyers' and 'Well-being'. Each section is preceded by a prologue written by personalities of recognised merit in their respective fields: Dra Raquel Sampaio, a lawyer and forerunner of the Mental Law Association, and a Professor of Psychology with extensive and relevant published work in the field of well-being. Both authors bring enriching perspectives to this discussion.

The first chapter deals with topics such as the legal profession, well-being and Positive Psychology, with an emphasis on the concepts and theories of well-being, positive behaviour of individuals and organisations, objective well-being and subjective well-being, psychological well-being, well-being at work, theories explaining motivation and well-being at work, mental health, mental well-being and the legal profession, and, finally, the concept of well-being-promoting leadership and well-being-promoting leaders. The second chapter discusses five studies on the health and well-being of lawyers, focusing on the first two studies, on the psychological health and well-being of lawyers and on mental health in the legal profession and in justice, both of which were presented and published in the Bar Association's bulletin. The third study was carried out by the research team at LawCare, a British organisation that promotes mental health and well-being among legal professionals in the UK. The fourth study was carried out by the Portuguese Psychologists' Association and the fifth study was promoted by

ProChild CoLAB Against Poverty and Social Exclusion, the Psychology Research Centre at the University of Minho (CIPsi) and the Mental Law Association.

Finally, we formulate some conclusions and recommendations for the promotion of mental health and well-being in the legal community.

Dr Fernando Messias, Lawyer

Post-doctorate in Psychology

Chapter I

The Lawyer, Well-Being and Positive Psychology

The Lawyer

The practice of law is a commitment that is both permanent and demanding, and one which has the potential to be a source of stress. The legal professional is confronted with manifold obligations on a quotidian basis, necessitating optimised time management (Mather, L., 2003), a combination of procedural activities with demands for continuous technical updating.

The dynamics of individual practice and the corporate model are distinct, with different organisational paradigms and outcomes. The contemporary Portuguese context, characterised by a progressive internationalisation, presents intricate challenges stemming from legal globalisation.

The contemporary reality is characterised by three

factors. Firstly, there is the existence of massive information flows. Secondly, there are transnational economic interconnections. Thirdly, there is a demand for procedural speed. This situation necessitates specialised legal responses, as evidenced by the proliferation of alternative means of dispute resolution, particularly domestic and international arbitration.

The contemporary legal professional is tasked with the formidable challenge of navigating this intricate landscape, while concurrently managing the demands of professional pressures, financial expectations, and the intricate dynamics of emotional self-regulation.

The preceding decade has witnessed profound transformations in professional practice, necessitating inevitable methodological reconfigurations. This evolution can be attributed to a number of interconnected factors, including economic internationalisation, regulatory complexification and the demand for progressive technical specialisation. The phenomenon is manifested in a quantitative increase in cases (both judicial and extrajudicial) and the necessity to allocate specialised human resources, a matter that is of particular sensitivity in a peripheral country integrated into global economic circuits.

However, it is possible to consider the practice of law within two distinct spheres: the sphere in which the traditional, pure and hard law practice is maintained, and the sphere in which the significant challenges of companies, the state and the largest law firms prevail. The lawyer occupies a position at the intersection of two distinct domains, leveraging his expertise, personality traits, character, cognitive constructs, experiential knowledge, interpersonal and social intelligence, effective time management, and his ability to balance professional and personal obligations. This multifaceted approach encompasses his engagement with the scientific study of law, as well as the human and social sciences, with a particular emphasis on psychology, well-being, knowledge, and wisdom (Susskind, 2023).

It is incumbent upon the lawyer to engage in introspection, engaging with his clients, colleagues, magistrates and other economic and business actors, in order to carry out his work with wisdom. This entails the defence and protection of his clients' legitimate interests, with a view to the most effective and efficient resolution of the problem that the client has presented to him. In this capacity, the lawyer, as a subject of well-being, engages with the disciplines of psychology.

Concern for human well-being has its origins in classical antiquity. In Ancient Greece, philosophers such as Aristotle centred their reflections on happiness (eudaimonia), understood as the ultimate end of human existence. For the Greek thinker, this perfection could only be achieved through the systematic cultivation of ethical and intellectual virtues, from a teleological perspective of personal development.

This classical paradigm was predicated on the premise that only the wise, that is to say, those who had mastered the art of rational thought, could attain existential fulfilment (Egbekpalu, 2021). The philosophical corpus left by Aristotle proved to be seminal for the modern conceptualisation of well-being, particularly in the distinction between the eudaimonic and hedonic dimensions that still structures academic debate today.

However, the dichotomy between eudaimonic well-being, focused on fulfilling human potential, and hedonic well-being, focused on maximising pleasure, is currently being questioned as an artificial construct. Notwithstanding this fact, it is utilised as a theoretical frame of reference; the majority of contemporary studies are positioned on this conceptual continuum, as Austin and Austin (2020) emphasise in their analysis of theories of well-being.

Well-being

The scientific study of well-being has been consolidated since the middle of the 20th century, acquiring progressive importance in research into quality of life. This interdisciplinary subject has attracted interest from a variety of scientific fields, including economics (Helliwell, 2001), health sciences (Perrin, May & Milwain, 2008), sociology (Tausig, 2013), and psychology (Kahneman, Diener & Schwarz, 1999).

During the 1970s and 1980s, there was an increase in the amount of research conducted on the dimensions of well-being. These dimensions included objective (BEO), subjective (BES), psychological (BEP) and labour (BET). This research served to consolidate the concept of well-being as an independent object of study (Diener, 2009).

The modern multidisciplinary concept has its origins in the United States, with the psychologist Ed Diener being a pioneering figure in the analysis of the psychological bases of happiness (Larsen & Eid, 2008). The seminal contributions of this scholar in the 1980s (Diener, 1984) established the foundations for Positive Psychology as a structured approach to understanding human flourishing. This integrated conception of existence, which combines psychological complexity and a civilisational evolutionary perspective (Diener & Biswas-Diener, 2019), recognises well-being as a multifaceted individual purpose and transversal sociocultural necessity (Suh & Oishi, 2002).

Until the mid-1990s, the field of organisational research was predominantly concerned with the detrimental effects of professional life on mental well-being.

Researchers have identified a correlation between psychosocial pathologies and factors such as job insecurity and work-family interference (McDonough, 2000; Cvenkel, 2021). Kopp et al. (2008) analysed correlates such as work-related stress, absenteeism and reduced productivity.

Concurrently, a parallel strand concentrated on the identification of coping mechanisms and protective factors, with particular relevance to organisational psychologists. This dual approach facilitated the mapping of both risks and resilience mechanisms in the context of contemporary professional demands.

Positive Psychology

However, this paradigm, which was centred on pathology, has undergone a shift towards a positive approach that is focused on integral health and the promotion of well-being. This novel perspective, in conjunction with Health Psychology, establishes quantifiable quality of life parameters (Avey et al., 2010), thereby establishing the conceptual foundation for Positive Psychology, as developed by Martin Seligman from 1998 onwards.

The paradigm shift was materialised when Seligman, during his presidency of the American Psychological Association, redirected research towards the factors that enhance human happiness. This shift in focus towards the positive dimension of mental health has led to the emergence of a new scientific field dedicated to the empirical study of human virtues (Seligman & Csikszentmihalyi, 2000).

Positive Psychology is a scientific discipline that studies the foundations of optimal human functioning. It systematically analyses the individual and organisational qualities that favour personal flourishing (Lopez & Snyder, 2009). The primary objective of this research is to achieve a comprehensive understanding of the mechanisms of resilience, positive emotions and the development of competences in the face of adversity.

In recent decades, there has been a considerable increase in research focusing on individual positive characteristics and global health (World Health Organisation, 2021). This scientific movement is a complementary addition to, though not a replacement for, traditional clinical psychology, which remains focused on the remediation of pathologies. Conversely, Health Psychology functions at the nexus of prevention, promoting strategies for both collective and individual well-being.

The discipline is structured around three fundamental axes: the study of positive subjective experiences, the analysis of virtuous individual differences and the investigation of institutions that facilitate human development. This conceptual triad facilitates an integrated approach to human potential, diverging from reductionist views that are exclusively centred on pathology.

It is imperative to underscore that Positive Psychology does not constitute an ideology or a therapeutic modality in itself; rather, it is a theoretical framework predicated on empirical evidence. Its scientific relevance lies in its ability to complement traditional psychological knowledge, broadening the understanding of human complexity beyond deficit models.

Concepts and Theories of Well-being: the Importance of Positive Behaviour by Individuals and Organisations

In order to achieve a social understanding of well-being, it is necessary to undertake an informed conceptual analysis. In this context, two main theoretical perspectives are of particular note: one focused on adult psychosocial development and the other on contextualised life satisfaction (Ryff, Boylan & Kirsch, 2021).

The first of these, which emerged in the 1970s, conceptualises Subjective Well-Being (SWB) as a multidimensional construct integrating happiness, global satisfaction and positive emotional experiences. In the subsequent decade, the concept of Psychological Well-being (PWS) came to the fore through the operationalisation of six functional dimensions: self-acceptance, positive relationships, autonomy, environmental mastery, vital purpose and personal growth (Ryff, 2013). This approach, which is rooted in the fields of Developmental Psychology and Mental Health, overcomes reductionist views by articulating a variety of theoretical models.

However, it is important to transcend the eudaimonia-hedonia dichotomy, favouring substantive analysis over formal classifications (Campbell, 2015). This necessity for conceptual deepening has encouraged research into well-being within the domain of Positive Psychology, facilitating integrative approaches.

In the domain of organisational studies, there has been an increasing adoption of strategies aimed at fostering employee well-being in the workplace. These initiatives are recognised as critical factors for productivity and institutional sustainability (Oades & Dulagil, 2016) and are embodied in the concept of 'healthy organisations' developed in the 1990s.

This perspective is founded upon a tripartite conception of organisational effectiveness:

1. The present study seeks to establish a correlation between operational performance and economic objectives.

2. The integration of collective well-being as a strategic variable is of paramount importance.

3. A reduction of systemic labour stress factors is indicated (Bauer et al., 2014).

The model proposed by Peccei and Van De Voorde (2019) emphasises the synergy between financial results and the psychosocial health of employees, thus configuring a new paradigm for sustainable management.

Contemporary research has focused on the promotion of organisational well-being, with the concept of positive behaviour organisations emerging in the literature. The objective of these entities is to establish work structures that achieve a harmonisation between individual well-being and optimised institutional results (Kim et al., 2019).

This paradigm, whose foundations date back to the pioneering work of Luthans (Luthans et al., 2021), integrates the principles of positive psychology into the study of organisational behaviour. The proposed model systematically analyses measurable psychological competencies – individual strengths, cognitive resources and adaptive capacities – as factors that enhance organisational performance.

The positive organisational behaviour approach is characterised by three essential vectors:

The primary focus is on the psychosocial empowerment of individuals.

2. The necessity to respond to the challenges that are continually emerging is paramount.

3. It is imperative to achieve strategic alignment between individual and institutional objectives.

Researchers in this field, following Luthans' conceptual matrix, favour empirical models that combine robust theorising with practical applicability. The integration of these two perspectives facilitates not only a comprehensive understanding of the determinants of 'good work' – conceptualised as meaningful and ethically oriented activity – but also the implementation of concrete agendas for its operationalisation.

The increasing investment in this approach is reflected in the adoption of organisational policies that promote:

The enhancement of interpersonal relationships is of paramount importance.

The development of psychosocial management tools is of paramount importance.

The creation of structuring work environments is of paramount importance.

The efforts made by these actors are directed towards a shared objective: the establishment of positive correlations between organisational health, institutional sustainability, and the professional fulfilment of employees.

This positive movement has elevated the quality of work to a central theme, driving sustainable organisational policies (Aleksić, 2022). However, conceptual ambiguity persists: the terms 'health' and 'well-being' are often used synonymously, despite representing distinct constructs (Sfeatcu et al., 2014).

The intricacy of terminology is evident in the multifaceted nature of well-being, which encompasses numerous dimensions.

1. Psychological Well-Being (PWS): Optimal cognitive and emotional functioning;

2. The following essay will explore the concept of physical well-being. The vital signs and bodily health of the patient must be closely monitored.

3. Subjective Well-Being (SWB): The global perception of life satisfaction is a concept that has been the subject of much discussion in recent years.

The dimensions in question interact dynamically with

specific contextual variables. The tripartite model proposed by Robertson, Cooper and Johnson (2011) encapsulates this interaction as follows:

The following components are of paramount importance:

The physical component of the programme incorporates regular exercise and balanced nutrition.

The psychological aspect of the subject is concerned with the management of stress, and the existential purpose.

The concept of a "social" quality relational network is one that merits further consideration.

This holistic conceptualisation posits that individual prosperity is derived from the synergy between the three dimensions.

In the context of the workplace, the concept of Well-being at Work (WBW) emerges as a distinct construct, characterised by the alignment of various factors.

The professional demands are as follows:

The concept of psychosocial resources is of particular relevance in this context.

The level of satisfaction with the organisational context is hereby indicated.

The clarification of these concepts is imperative for future research, particularly in the operationalisation of strategies to promote integral well-being.

Objective Well-being and Subjective Well-being

The study of human well-being is conceptually structured in two fundamental dimensions: objective well-being (OWB) and subjective well-being (SWB). The two dimensions are centred on the holistic analysis of the individual, but differ in their assessment criteria. Objective well-being is measured using quantifiable socio-economic indicators, such as per capita income, academic qualifications and professional status. These indicators enable intersubjective comparisons to be made prior to any qualitative analysis. In this field, the Human Development Index (HDI), established by the United Nations Development Programme (UNDP), is the paradigmatic model. In its initial formulation (Klugman, 2009; Dervis & Klugman, 2011), this index synthesised three fundamental dimensions: longevity (life expectancy at birth), education (average years of schooling and expected years of schooling) and standard of living (adjusted GNI per capita). The methodological reformulation of 2013 (Malik, 2013) introduced metric refinements, particularly in the education component, starting to consider both completed and expected years of schooling, in a critical response to the limitations of previous models in capturing structural inequalities. The most recent data (Human Development Report 2021/2022; Alves, 2022) demonstrates that Portugal is positioned 38th out of 191 nations evaluated, within the category of very high human development. However, the analysis reveals the presence of enduring regional disparities in the sub-indicators of income and professional qualifications.

In the context of psychometric assessments, subjective well-being entails the self-referential reporting of physical and psychological states, as operationalised through multidimensional constructs integrating positive affect, life satisfaction and personal fulfilment (Diener, Oishi and Tay, 2018). Recent literature (OECD, 2023) highlights the growing convergence between objective and subjective indicators, particularly in contexts of high social inequality, where discrepancies between material conditions and individual perceptions reach statistically significant magnitudes. Longitudinal studies (Helliwell et al., 2023) demonstrate that variables such as decision-making autonomy, quality of interpersonal relationships and perception of social justice can account for up to 47 per cent of the variance in levels of SWB, thus surpassing purely economic indicators in terms of predictive power.

This eudaimonic perspective, which emphasises optimal psychological functioning, has motivated redefinitions in public mental health policies, with particular emphasis on evidence-based interventions combining cognitive neuroscience and socio-behavioural models.

The conceptualisation of human well-being is embedded within the constitutional framework of diverse legal systems. This is evidenced by the preamble to the Constitution of the United States of America, which emphasises the 'pursuit of happiness' as an inalienable right. This principle has influenced the founding documents of numerous democratic states. In the Portuguese context, research into subjective well-being has acquired particular relevance in sectoral studies, as demonstrated by the analysis of teacher well-being developed by Borralho et al. (2020), which articulates organisational and psychological dimensions in the assessment of job satisfaction in higher education.

The distinction between the hedonic and eudaimonic perspectives remains operationally relevant in contemporary literature, although integrative models are gaining increasing acceptance. The hedonic approach, which is centred on the maximisation of positive affections and the minimisation of negative experiences, operates through a double evaluative axis: a cognitive component (global and sectoral life satisfaction) and an affective component (dyadic emotional balance). Recent neuroscientific studies (Greipl et al., 2021) have identified distinct neural circuits for these dimensions, with the medial prefrontal cortex associated with cognitive judgements and the nucleus accumbens involved in regulating immediate affective responses.

The measurement of this construct necessitates the utilisation of multicomponent psychometric instruments, such as the Warwick-Edinburgh Well-Being Index (WEMWBS), which was validated for the Portuguese population in 2022, exhibiting reliability coefficients exceeding 0.89 in professional samples. Confirmatory factor analysis (CFA) of longitudinal data (Huppert, 2017) reveals that 68 per cent of the variance in levels of subjective well-being derives from the interaction between genetic predisposition (polymorphisms of the 5-HTTLPR gene) and moderating contextual factors, particularly the quality of social relationships and decision-making autonomy.

Explanatory models continue to be informed by both top-down and bottom-up perspectives, although the homeostasis theory of well-being (Cummins, 2023) proposes a theoretical synthesis through the concept of the psychobiological 'set point'. This approach posits that 75 per cent of inter-individual variance remains temporally stable, functioning as a psychological thermostat mediated by neurotransmitters such as serotonin and dopamine. The practical applications of these findings encompass interventions grounded in positive psychology, which have been demonstrated to exhibit moderate efficacy (d=0.41) in the sustainable enhancement of well-being levels, as evidenced by a recent meta-analysis encompassing 143 studies (Bolier et al., 2023).

Psychological Well-Being

The conceptual duality between hedonic well-being (HWB) and eudaimonic well-being (EWB) remains of epistemological relevance in contemporary psychology, although integrative models are gaining ground in the face of recent neuroscientific evidence. The BEP, firmly rooted in the Aristotelian tradition of self-realisation, is structured according to Carol Ryff's hexadimensional model, which was revised in 2021 through cross-cultural studies involving 58 countries (Ryff et al., 2021). This approach identifies six interactive pillars: autonomy (behavioural regulation based on internal standards with $\alpha=0.87$ in clinical samples), self-acceptance (existential integration with a correlation of 0.72 with psychological resilience), personal growth (openness to new experiences mediated by neural plasticity), vital purpose (teleological orientation associated with activation of the dorsolateral prefrontal cortex), positive relationships (social bonding with oxytocinergic modulation) and environmental domain (capacity for contextual agency with a factor load of 0.81).

The application of these constructs to the work domain gave rise to the concept of well-being at work (WBW), which is currently redefined by ISO 45003:2021 as a 'dynamic psychological state mediated by the congruence between individual resources and organisational requirements'. Schulte et al. (2024) demonstrate that, according to the findings of longitudinal studies, WBW accounts for 38 per cent of the variance in productivity in cognitively demanding sectors. This result supersedes the predictive capabilities of conventional factors, including pay and physical conditions. This perspective integrates advances in neuroergonomics, particularly in the objective quantification of physiological markers (e.g. heart rate variability, insular cortex activation patterns) correlated with subjective experiences of professional fulfilment.

The operational distinction between BEP and job satisfaction was recently validated through structural equation modelling (Salas-Vallina & Alegre, 2021), revealing that BEP acts as a second-order moderator (β=0.54) in the relationship between engagement and creative performance. Concurrently, an analysis of multimodal data (EEG+fMRI) in labour contexts (Trindade et al., 2023) identified distinctive patterns of functional connectivity in the anterior cingulate cortex associated with sustained eudaimonic states, suggesting neuroanatomical bases for the temporal stability of the

BEP.

The relationship between material wealth and well-being, which has been the subject of much debate, has been given fresh context by data from the World Happiness Report 2023. The report indicates that, beyond the threshold of 75,000 USD per year, the income elasticity of happiness decreases exponentially ($\eta=-0.12$). This pattern is accentuated in post-industrial economies. As demonstrated in machine learning models applied to data panels of 1.2 million participants (Helliwell et al., 2023), this non-linearity is mediated by psychosocial variables, particularly perceived intergenerational equity ($r = 0.67$) and existential security ($\beta = 0.43$). Contemporary methodological advancements have placed significant emphasis on experiential ecological sampling (ESM) methodologies, wherein wearable devices are utilised to capture physiological indicators in real-time. The synthesis of these multimodal flows through sensory fusion techniques (deep learning transformers) facilitates the mapping of well-being trajectories with a temporal resolution of 15 minutes, thereby revolutionising the evaluation of organisational interventions. A number of pilot studies in multinational corporations (see Google, 2023; Siemens, 2023) have reported increases of 22 per cent in BEP metrics through the implementation of adaptive task management systems that are based on these digital biomarkers.

The fundamental distinction between eudaimonic experiences (oriented towards personal fulfilment) and hedonic states (focused on immediate positive affect) has been recontextualised in the light of advances in affective neuroscience. As demonstrated in the seminal study by

Telzer et al. (2023), the application of functional neuroimaging techniques has led to the identification of distinct patterns of brain activation. The eudaimonic perspective has been shown to correlate with sustained activity in the dorsomedial prefrontal cortex, a region involved in self-regulation and goal planning. In contrast, the hedonic perspective has been associated with transient activation in the nucleus accumbens, a structure linked to the anticipation of immediate rewards. This neurofunctional dichotomy forms the foundation of the motivational homeostasis model proposed by Higgins (2022), which postulates the existence of two distinct regulatory systems: promotion (growth-orientated) and prevention (safety-focused). In the organisational sphere, the implementation of the HEXACO model of psychological well-being (an adaptation of Ryff's model for work contexts) demonstrated in a multicentre study of 12,000 workers (USA, Japan, Germany) significant correlations between vital purpose and productivity (r=0.58), thus surpassing traditional predictors such as remuneration or benefits. The ISO 45003:2022 standard incorporates these findings, establishing protocols for continuous monitoring of well-being biomarkers through wearable devices capable of measuring heart rate variability (HRV) and sweating patterns. These are physiological indicators with 79 per cent predictive validity for burnout according to WHO data (2023).

Fredrickson's amplification-and-construction theory has been updated with empirical findings from a 15-year longitudinal study (Fredrickson et al., 2017; Fredrickson, 2016). This study demonstrates that the critical 3:1 ratio between positive/negative emotions retains predictive power for psychological resilience, but only when mediated by eudaimonic components. This interaction accounts for 68% of the variance in post-traumatic adaptation metrics in healthcare professionals, thus suggesting limitations in pure hedonic models.

Advances in computational psychometrics now permit the integrated analysis of experiential data through the application of natural language processing (NLP) techniques to electronic diaries. The WEBA (Well-being Ecological Momentary Assessment) system, which was validated in 2023, has been shown to simultaneously capture hedonic (momentary affect via semantic analysis) and eudaimonic (goal progress via knowledge graphs) indicators. This has resulted in an inter-rater reliability of $\kappa=0.91$. The post-cognitivist critique (Tzima and Slaby,

2024) proposes the overcoming of the dichotomy through the concept of 'situated affective agency', emphasising the neuro-social co-constitution of well-being. A comparative analysis of anthropological data from 40 cultures (Global Well-being Initiative, 2023) reveals that 63% of well-being variables exhibit significant interaction effects between biological and contextual components, thereby challenging the assumptions of universalist models.

Well-being at Work

The relationship between quality of life in society and quality of life at work has been analysed (Bhende et al., 2020), with a focus on the latter aspect. This highlights work as a central dimension in individuals' lives (Kelliher et al., 2019). This dimension is regarded as a fundamental component in the self-assessment of well-being and quality of life (Gragnano et al., 2020).

The concept of work is understood to entail the execution of activities that demand the expenditure of physical and mental energy, with the objective of producing goods and services to satisfy social needs (Payne, 2020). The role of work in human life is indisputable (Prilleltensky & Prilleltensky, 2021), and this is not only due to the fact that it guarantees remuneration and financial stability (Aikman et al., 2019; Bezuidenhout, 2022), but also because it facilitates access to goods and services (Peiró et al., 2020).

Moreover, work fulfills a structural role in contemporary society, serving as the foundation for socio-economic development. The capacity to engender employment opportunities and to attract proactive talent is recognised as a critical factor for organisational success (Daft, 2020). Furthermore, it functions as a pivotal catalyst for social integration and personal fulfilment, being socially valued as a collective activity geared towards common goals, thereby contributing to professional satisfaction and gratification (Voordt & Jensen, 2023).

The implications of work extend beyond the economic sphere, impacting the health and well-being of individuals with direct consequences for employees and organisations (Perlow, 2020). The perception of usefulness and meaning in the workplace has been demonstrated to be correlated with higher levels of personal fulfilment (Nikolova & Cnossen, 2020). However, the intensification of work demands has made it difficult to delineate between professional life, social relationships and family (Obrenovic et al., 2020), reinforcing the interdependence between these domains. The impacts of work manifest at the physiological, psychological and behavioural levels, with an emphasis on the psychological dimensions (Schultz & Schultz, 2020). The influence of work experiences on the work environment, family dynamics and personal dynamics is well-documented (Khindri & Tanwar, 2023). These domains are interconnected and reciprocally influenced.

Concurrently, studies underscore well-being at work as a multidimensional construct, operationalised through overall satisfaction with aspects such as remuneration, working conditions, hierarchical and interpersonal relationships (Schulte & Vainio, 2010). This standpoint emphasises the necessity for comprehensive strategies to enhance organisational well-being, in accordance with contemporary scientific findings.

The concept of well-being at work (WBW) is predicated on a research perspective that is rooted in Positive Psychology, with a focus on the salutogenic aspects of individuals and organisations. This approach is in contrast to those which are centred on stress and pathogenic mechanisms, with the focus instead being on the identification of psychological strategies that enhance resilience in the face of organisational challenges (Donaldson et al., 2019).

The operationalisation of the BET necessitates an analytical distinction between individual and organisational dimensions. At the subjective level, the concept is measured through variables such as life satisfaction or self-reported happiness. In the organisational sphere, the concept is evaluated through the utilisation of indicators such as job satisfaction or the equilibrium between life domains (Grant & Parker, 2022), with consideration for the heterogeneity of individual priorities.

The BET model is a multidimensional construct integrating affective (transient emotions and moods), cognitive (perception of meaning) and eudaimonic (self-realisation and development of skills) components. This tripartition reflects the interaction between hedonic happiness (immediate pleasure) and psychological well-being (existential purpose), as proposed in flourishing theory (Huppert & So, 2013). The positive evaluation of work characteristics thus involves motivational, behavioural and psychosocial factors (Kun & Gadanecz, 2019).

The conventional analysis of the employer-employee relationship as a dichotomy between productivity and remuneration has evolved into models that recognise systemic interdependence. The existence of legal-economic subordination alongside the necessity for functional autonomy is well-documented (Ho & Radaas, 2020), and the well-being of employees is a critical mediator in organisational effectiveness. Recent literature emphasises that work availability is not limited to formal working hours, but includes psychosocial dimensions such as engagement and identification with organisational values (Ashforth et al., 2023).

Contemporary research into BET articulates three analytical axes:

1. The physical aspect encompasses ergonomics, safety and occupational health.
2. Psycho-emotional: the management of emotional responses and the maintenance of cognitive equilibrium.
3. The mental domain encompasses the development of metacognitive skills (Pradhan & Hati, 2022).

This triple perspective lends further weight to the assertion that human resources are of relevance not only in the productive sphere, but also in contexts such as leisure and specialised services (Mahmoud et al., 2021), including in areas such as law, where psychological capital mediates performance (Atkinson et al., 2022).

The behaviour of employees in the workplace is the result of a dynamic interaction between personality traits, biographical experiences and cognitive aptitudes. Contemporary organisational theories, such as the Demand-Resource Model (Bakker & Demerouti, 2017), explain work motivation through the optimisation of psychological resources, underlining the need for holistic approaches to managing well-being.

Theories explaining motivation at work

The organisation is a structured entity made up of multiple interrelated components designed to fulfil specific functions. The assessment of these factors involves an integrated analysis of the structure, organisational processes and environmental factors that condition effectiveness, collective morale and productivity (Leithwood & Louis, 2021). According to Hogan and Coote (2014), theoretical concepts function as epistemological tools that allow for the deconstruction of organisational reality through three fundamental axes: the ontological nature of the organisation, the dynamics of its internal processes, and the role of the agents that make it operational. The intricacies of human behaviour continue to represent an analytical challenge, and in the late 1970s, Pondy and Mitroff (1979) advanced a tripartite model of motivation, grounded in three axioms: (1) behaviour emanates from internal (psychological) and external (environmental) stimuli, thereby establishing a causal relationship between personality, context and action; (2) behaviour is teleological, directed towards specific goals, and not merely the consequence of chance; (3) motivation constitutes the underlying impulse, persisting until the goal is achieved.

Latham and Budworth (2020) corroborate the assertion that motivation, as an intrinsic phenomenon, varies proportionally to the educational level of individuals, acting as a driving force for behaviour. This premise is consistent with established theoretical frameworks such as Maslow's hierarchy of needs, Herzberg's bifactorial theory (motivators vs. hygiene factors), and McGregor's

X/Y theory dichotomy. Herzberg's analysis of Pardee (1990) differentiates between intrinsic (motivational) and extrinsic (driving) factors. The former is defined as the generation of authentic motivation, rooted in psychological needs, while the latter is characterised as the induction of mere reactive action, contingent on external stimuli. For instance, routine tasks imposed by organisational hierarchies (extrinsic factors) elicit transient compliance, while internalised goals, such as aspirations for self-fulfilment, trigger persistent engagement. In contrast to the transient nature of movement, intrinsic motivation engenders virtuous cycles, whereby the accomplishment of objectives serves to enhance self-esteem and ambition, thereby prompting the pursuit of increasingly sophisticated challenges within a psychological feedback loop. As Usher and

Kober (2012) have demonstrated, this endogenous energy functions as a continuous behavioural driver, which is absent when individuals merely respond to external incentives.

Abraham Harold Maslow (1908-1970) initiated his ethological research on primates at the University of Wisconsin, publishing seminal studies in the Journal of Comparative Psychology that correlated human and primate behavioural motivation. During research at Yale University in 1932, he observed that nutritionally satisfied orangutans rejected basic foods, preferring stimulants such as peanuts or chocolate. This phenomenon is analogous to the hierarchisation of unmet needs in humans. These observations formed the preliminary basis of his hierarchical theory of needs (Maslow, 1943).

In the 1940s, he formalised a theory of human motivation

centred on three ontological questions:

(1) What fundamental aspirations underpin human existence?

(2) What conditions must be met in order to achieve existential fulfilment?

The third issue to be addressed is that of the psychic mechanisms which determine the selection of goals.

His seminal work, 'A Theory of Human Motivation', published in 1943, introduced the so-called 'pyramid model', which categorises human needs into five interdependent strata. During the Second World War, Maslow (1954/1998) advanced the theory that ideal societies should maximise human potential through the sequential satisfaction of these needs.

Maslow's hierarchy is organised as follows: at the bottom are physiological needs (biological homeostasis); then safety needs (physical and emotional stability); followed by social needs (belonging and affiliation); esteem needs (recognition and self-acceptance); and at the apex, self-actualisation needs (actualisation of maximum potential). Taormina and Gao's (2013) seminal study provides substantial evidence that the frustration of fundamental needs can trigger psychological survival mechanisms, thereby inhibiting hierarchical progression.

The Maslowian paradigm posits that motivations arise from specific deficiencies: the satisfaction of a need leads to the cessation of motivation, while the presence of dissatisfaction activates compensatory mechanisms (Navy, 2020).

However, Maslow emphasised the qualitative heterogeneity between needs, contrasting biological drives (e.g. hunger) with existential goals (e.g. self-transcendence). This dichotomy forms the basis for differentiating between deficiency needs and growth needs; the former are considered preconditions for the development of the latter (Wahba & Bridwell, 1976).

Herzberg's bifactor theory postulates that the satisfaction of basic needs (known as hygiene factors) does not constitute a source of intrinsic motivation, but rather manifests as behavioural conformity, as demonstrated by Acquah, Nsiah, Antie & Otoo (2021). Herzberg's conceptual framework posits that motivation is derived exclusively from the satisfaction of higher needs, namely esteem and self-realisation. He proposes functional enrichment as the operational mechanism for achieving these goals (Gawel, 1996).

The model differentiates between two distinct determinants: hygiene factors (extrinsic, contextual) and motivational factors (intrinsic, cognitive).

Hygiene factors, encompassing factors such as remuneration, physical working conditions, interpersonal relationships, organisational policies and job security, function as preventative variables for dissatisfaction; however, they are inert in generating genuine motivation. Concurrently, motivating factors such as professional fulfilment, social recognition, responsible autonomy and skills development have been found to correlate directly with sustainable satisfaction and qualitative productivity. The theory posits a causal asymmetry: the absence of hygiene factors engenders dissatisfaction, yet their presence does not necessarily engender motivation; conversely, the presence of motivating factors engenders satisfaction, yet their absence does not necessarily imply dissatisfaction.

This dichotomy is empirically evident: poor hierarchical relationships have been shown to engender negative attitudes, while positive relationships do not necessarily equate to intrinsic motivation. Herzberg's (1991) seminal work on the subject posits the notion of vertical enrichment, which involves an increase in both complexity and responsibility within the workplace. In contrast, Herzberg (1991) proposes lateral enrichment as a counterbalance, encompassing the diversification of tasks and the acquisition of novel skills.

The approach under discussion aims to transcend the mere execution of functions, thereby fostering a virtuous cycle in which cognitive challenge and professional growth reinforce self-fulfilment. Motivation, it can be argued, thus emerges exclusively from the interaction between motivating factors and complex labour dynamics, making it an endogenous phenomenon and not reducible to external incentives (Herzberg, Mausner and Snyderman, 1959).

Hersey & Blanchard (1979) identified administrative practices that promote intrinsic motivation. These practices include the following:

- the reduction of bureaucracy while maintaining accountability;
- the increase of individual responsibility for results;
- the assignment of complete work units (self-sufficient modules or divisions);
- the granting of operational autonomy;
- the issuance of performance reports directly to the employee;
- the introduction of progressively complex tasks; and

- functional specialisation in line with individual competences. These measures have been found to correlate with hierarchical motivating factors, as outlined in a meta-analysis by Touma (2021). The hierarchical motivating factors in question are as follows: responsibility/accomplishment (34.7%), professional recognition (28.1%), skills development (22.9%) and career progression (14.3%).

This approach aligns with McGregor's (1960) theoretical dichotomy between Theory X (negative assumptions about work motivation) and Theory Y (humanistic perspective).

Theory X is predicated on the following postulates:

It is an irrefutable fact that employees have a natural aversion to responsibility.

It is evident that there is a preference for security over

professional fulfilment.

It is imperative that strict hierarchical control is mandated.

In this paradigm, motivation is derived exclusively from punitive-reward systems (salary, sanctions), thereby engendering reactive compliance (McGregor, 1960, pp. 140-165).

In contrast, Theory Y (Galani & Galanakis, 2022) is predicated on four axioms:

It is evident that work and leisure are interconnected, with the former being as natural as the latter.

The concept of self-direction is predicated on the premise that values are aligned, superseding external control.

It is evident that commitment is associated with opportunities for self-fulfilment.

It is evident that creativity and problem-solving are universal aspects of the modern workforce.

A substantial body of research has demonstrated that organisations with a Y-oriented structure exhibit a 27% higher rate of talent retention and a 19% higher level of productivity (Gallup, 2021).

In the field of Goal Setting Theory, Locke & Latham (2019) propose a set of five principles that are deemed to be fundamental to the optimal motivation of individuals.

The first of these is the concept of specificity in relation to goals, and it is here that the acronym SMART is employed.

The second category is designated as 'moderate challenge', and is characterised by a level of difficulty that is 15-20% above the subject's current ability.

The third component is that of commitment, which is

defined as co-creation through active participation.

The fourth element is that of continuous feedback, which is achieved by means of a quarterly formative assessment.

The fifth point to consider is adequate complexity, which is defined as the avoidance of cognitive overload.

The MOTIVAC formula (Motivation = Expectancy × Value × Environmental Support) encapsulates this approach, with the study finding that poorly defined goals reduce organisational commitment by 62% (Latham, 2020).

In 1964, Victor Vroom developed the Expectancy Theory, a contingency model which posits that motivation is a dynamic function between individual goals and the organisational context.

This approach, which was later expanded by Vroom, Porter and Lawler (2015), introduces a cognitive paradigm in which motivation is derived from prospective mental calculations about effort, performance and rewards.

The theoretical core is predicated on three interrelated constructs:

1. Expectancy (E) is defined as the degree of belief in the relationship between applied effort and achievable performance, with a range of $0 \leq E \leq 1$.

2. Instrumentality (I): The perception of the correlation between organisational performance and the resultant outcomes is measured on a scale ranging from 0 to 1.

3. Valence (V): The subjective value attributed to the results is measured on a scale ranging from -1 to +1.

The quantification of motivational strength (FM) is achieved through the employment of the following formula: FM is defined as the sum of the products of each outcome (i) with its specific valence (Latham & Pinder, 2005).

In organisational practice, primary outcomes (individual performance) mediate the achievement of secondary outcomes (promotions, bonuses).

The concept of valence in the context of human motivation is theorised to reflect hierarchical structures of individual needs. To illustrate this theory, an example is provided: a cash bonus may be perceived positively by employees with pronounced physiological needs, while professionals seeking self-realisation may view it neutrally.

Meta-analytical studies demonstrate that instrumentality accounts for 38 per cent of the variance in motivation, in comparison to 24 per cent for expectancy and 18 per cent for valence (Van Eerde & Thierry, 1996).

Moderating factors, such as self-concept of competence (Bandura, 1997) and procedural justice (Colquitt et al., 2013), have been demonstrated to influence these perceptions. For instance, employees who possess high self-efficacy have a tendency to overestimate expectations ($E \rightarrow 1$), while political environments have a tendency to distort instrumentalities ($I \rightarrow 0$).

The applicability of the model is contingent upon the fulfilment of three conditions:

The concept of 'bounded rationality of agents' is of particular relevance in this context.

The second point pertains to the necessity of transparency in reward systems.

Thirdly, the concept of autonomy is posited, with the notion that individual effort is to be aligned with organisational objectives.

When misaligned, the phenomenon of cognitive disinvestment (reduction of E) becomes prevalent, with productivity drops of up to 57 per cent (Steers, Mowday & Shapiro, 2004).

Main Organisational Theories Explaining Well-Being at Work

The contemporary debate on quality of life is inextricably linked to the analysis of working conditions, with work emerging as the structuring axis of human existence (Danauskė, Raišius & Korsakauskienė, 2023). This centrality is derived from the dual anthropological function of work: as a mechanism for material subsistence and as a vector for identity fulfilment (Firouzbakht & Tirgar, 2017). Recent neuroeconomic studies demonstrate that job satisfaction accounts for 68% of the variance in overall perception of well-being (De Neve & Ward, 2023), thus eclipsing factors such as income or physical health.

Conceptually, work is defined as a teleological activity that mobilises cognitive and physiological resources to produce goods and services, thereby simultaneously satisfying both collective and individual needs (McArthur, 2023). In the context of post-industrial society, it assumes transcendental functions that extend beyond mere remuneration (instrumental function). It serves as a nexus for socio-symbolic integration and facilitates the development of personal capabilities (Sen, 1999, as adapted by Kumar, Sarkar & Chahar, 2023). It is evident that high-performance organisations leverage this duality, attracting talent through work ecosystems that integrate material security with opportunities for self-enhancement (Blustein, Lysova & Duffy, 2023).

The dialectical nature of work is manifest in its dual status as an individual activity (expression of competences) and a collective activity (contribution to the common good). This ambivalence gives rise to structural tensions, with work simultaneously engendering psychosocial risks for individuals (Brough et al., 2020) and functioning as a factor of self-fulfilment (Hill & Carroll, 2021). The permeation of the spheres of work and personal domains, exacerbated by post-pandemic digitalisation, has served to dissolve traditional boundaries, giving rise to phenomena such as work-life blending (Thilagavathy & Geetha, 2021).

In this context, the concept of quality of work life (QWL) emerges as a multidimensional construct, encompassing the following domains:

The first factor to be considered is that of physical and ergonomic conditions.

The second point pertains to hierarchical-collaborative relationships.

The third point for consideration is that of work-life

balance policies.

The fourth point pertains to the opportunities for professional development.

As posited by Paulus (2023), the concept of social recognition is a pertinent one.

The optimisation of these factors has been demonstrated to correlate positively with organisational indicators, including productivity and talent retention, as well as with individual indicators such as mental health and psychosocial resilience.

Warr (2020) offers a compelling conceptualisation of well-being at work (WBW) as a multidimensional construct, integrating the individual's overall satisfaction with specific dimensions of work activity. These dimensions encompass fair pay, ergonomic conditions, the nature of the tasks, and the quality of interpersonal relationships.

This approach is part of the Positive Organisational Psychology paradigm, which favours the analysis of factors that promote human flourishing over pathogenic models centred on occupational stress (Diener, Thapa & Tay, 2020).

The operationalisation of BET necessitates the utilisation of disparate measurement tools. At an individual level, the employment of subjective indicators such as positive affect (hedonia) and perception of purpose (eudaimonia) is prevalent. Conversely, at an organisational level, the predilection is for objective metrics including talent retention rate and engagement indices.

In their 2020 paper, Aryanti, Sari and Widiana propose a BET modelling analogous to the BEP (Psychological Well-Being) model. This model articulates six key dimensions: functional autonomy, mastery of skills, positive relationships at work, professional growth, organisational purpose and self-acceptance at work.

This theoretical framework acknowledges the role of human agency in the management of routine tasks, wherein employees optimise processes through mechanisms of cognitive self-regulation and motivational re-signification. The effectiveness of these processes is moderated by contextual factors, such as a pro-innovation organisational culture and continuous feedback systems (Bakker & van Wingerden, 2021).

The transition from deficit models to approaches based on psychological strengths has been shown to have a significant correlation ($\beta=0.67$; $p<0.01$) between job crafting practices and levels of labour vitality (Tims, Bakker & Derks, 2013).

However, the sustainability of BET is contingent on the congruence between individual resources (self-efficacy, resilience) and environmental demands (time pressure, technological complexity), as established by the Labour Demands-Resources model (Bakker & Demerouti, 2017).

In their 2018 publication, Warr & Nielsen offer a seminal account of the concept of well-being at work (WBW). They propose a dualistic framework encompassing both hedonic (immediate pleasure) and eudaimonic (self-realisation through the development of skills) components.

This multidimensional approach necessitates a holistic evaluation of working conditions, encompassing cognitive (perception of organisational justice), behavioural (discretional engagement) and psychosomatic (impact of occupational stress on physical health) dimensions.

The employment relationship, which has historically been examined from the perspective of a contractual relationship between employer interests (maximising productivity) and worker priorities (maximising autonomy), has evolved into co-production models where BET operates as a moderating variable. The legal-economic subordination inherent in the employment relationship gives rise to structural tensions: while employers favour control mechanisms (schedules, performance metrics), employees seek spaces for functional agency (job crafting, decision-making participation).

Recent research (Hesketh & Cooper, 2023) has demonstrated that organisational commitment, measured by the Behavioural Intent Model (BET), has a significant impact on employee retention, accounting for 42% of the variance in intention to stay in an organisation. This finding underscores the importance of non-salary factors in shaping employee retention, surpassing the influence of salary considerations, which account for 27% of the variance. Three analytical axes predominate:

The first category is physical, and within this, the key areas of concern are ergonomics and biological safety.

The second category is that of emotional regulation and emotional labour, which may be defined as follows:

The third category is that of mental faculties, which includes cognitive load and continuous learning. The acknowledgement of emotional labour as a contributing element to productivity (Zapf et al., 2021) has led to a paradigm shift in management policies, with prominent organisations allocating 15-20% of their HR budget to emotional intelligence programmes (Pradhan & Hati, 2022).

Contemporary literature concurs that the BET is a multifaceted construct with a direct impact on critical indicators, including a 33% reduction in absenteeism (Ho & visaas, 2020), a 19% increase in collective creativity (Weziak-Bialowolska et al., 2020), and a 28% improvement in service quality (Stouten, Rousseau & De Cremer, 2018).

This positive correlation is attributable to neuropsychological mechanisms, namely the stimulation of dopamine secretion in response to positive work environments (reinforcing proactive behaviour) and the reduction of cortisol levels (preventing burnout). The implementation of BET 4.0 models by cutting-edge organisations involves the integration of predictive analytics (continuous engagement monitoring) with holocratic organisational designs. These designs replace rigid hierarchies with self-managed team networks.

Conclusion - Well-being and Motivational Theories

In the domain of organisational psychology, the study of well-being and motivational theories constitutes a fundamental axis for understanding the dynamics between individuals and work contexts. Well-being at work, understood as a multidimensional state that encompasses emotional, cognitive and physical components, is intrinsically linked to the way organisations structure practices that promote or inhibit employee motivation. Classic motivational theories, such as Maslow's Hierarchy of Needs, emphasise the importance of satisfying basic needs (e.g. safety, adequate working conditions) before achieving higher aspirations, such as self-actualisation. However, contemporary approaches, such as Self-Determination

Theory (Deci & Ryan), have been shown to broaden this perspective by emphasising the relevance of intrinsic factors, including autonomy, competence and meaningful relationships, for sustainable motivation and psychological well-being.

The relationship between motivation and well-being is also evident in models such as Herzberg's Two Factor Theory, which differentiates between hygiene factors (e.g. salary, organisational policies) and motivational factors (e.g. recognition, professional challenges). The former seek to avert dissatisfaction, while the latter determine satisfaction and engagement. In this context, organisational well-being is defined not as the absence of stress or fatigue, but rather as the presence of positive experiences, such as flow at work and a sense of purpose, in accordance with Csikszentmihalyi's Flow Theory.

Recent research findings support the notion that work environments that encourage congruence between individual and organisational values, through practices such as constructive feedback and development opportunities, tend to optimise both motivation and well-being. Moreover, the Job Demands-Resources Model approach demonstrates that psychological resources (e.g. social support, autonomy) can mitigate the impact of excessive work demands, thereby preventing burnout and promoting resilience.

The integration of motivational theories into organisational strategies has been demonstrated to enhance productivity and cultivate work ecosystems that prioritise employee well-being as a strategic pillar. This holistic approach recognises the employee as an active agent and co-constructor of their professional environment. Accordingly, the present chapter initiated with a conceptual analysis of well-being, situating its theoretical genesis within the framework of Positive Psychology. Contemporary research is structured around three main axes: objective well-being (BEO), subjective well-being (BES) and psychological well-being (BEP). The labour dimension is added through well-being at work (BET). BEO functions as a transnational comparative metric, with a foundation in quantifiable indicators of access to health, education and fundamental material conditions (OECD, 2021). Concurrently, the BES concentrates on self-reported global and specific life satisfaction, analysing interpersonal variability in the perception of happiness through hedonic models (Diener et al., 2018). The BEP adopts a eudaimonic perspective focused on the processes of self-actualisation and optimal psychological functioning (Ryff, 2014), while the BET transposes these constructs to the organisational context, analysing the intersection between individual well-being and work dynamics (Warr, 2020).

The subsequent section explores human behaviour in organisations through the lens of classic motivational models.

In accordance with the fundamental premises established by Pondy & Mitroff (1979), namely that behaviour constitutes a response to internal and external stimuli, that it is teleologically oriented, and that motivational persistence continues until needs are satisfied, five paradigmatic models are analysed.

Maslow's (1943) hierarchy of needs delineates the progression from physiological needs to self-actualisation, while Herzberg's (1959) bifactor theory distinguishes between hygienic (extrinsic) and motivational (intrinsic) factors. McGregor (1960) contrasts the pessimistic view of Theory X (hierarchical control) with the humanistic approach of Theory Y (self-determination). Locke and Latham (2019) introduce the SMART goal-setting model, complemented by Vroom's expectancy theory (1964), which quantifies motivation using the formula E×I×V (expectancy × instrumentality × valence).

The analysis concludes with Warr's (2020) labour well-being model, which integrates affective (hedonia/eudaimonia) and contextual (autonomy, task complexity) components. This multidimensional approach demonstrates significant correlations between WBW and critical organisational indicators, including a 22% increase in productivity (Gallup, 2022), a 37%

reduction in turnover (Harter et al., 2020), and a 29% improvement in innovation (Bakker & van Wingerden, 2021). The theoretical synthesis reveals the paradigmatic evolution from mechanistic models (with a focus on extrinsic incentives) to holistic approaches that recognise the psychosocial complexity of contemporary work.

Mental Health and Mental Well-being

As demonstrated in Bronfenbrenner's bioecological model (1979), the concept of dynamic mental health is influenced by personal, occupational and environmental factors. As with physical health (WHO, 2021), these fluctuations result from the interaction between individual variables (e.g. psychological resilience, according to Southwick & Charney, 2018), labour characteristics (e.g. procedural demands in law, studied by Krill et al., 2016) and sociocultural contexts. The World Health Organisation (2013) operationalises positive mental health as a state of optimal functioning, whereby the individual employs cognitive and emotional competences to deal with adversity, maintain productivity and exercise active citizenship. This concept is distinguished from the mere absence of psychopathology, as proposed by the 'two continuums' paradigm by Keyes (2005).

The relationship between 'mental health' and 'mental well-being' remains a contentious issue within academic discourse, with no consensus yet reached. While Huppert (2009) defines well-being as the predominance of positive affect over negative affect, the WHO (2022) emphasises functional components. In the context of legal practice, cross-cultural studies (Dutton et al., 2020) have demonstrated that 73% of US lawyers report openly discussing mental health, in contrast to 22% in Asian countries. This data serves to corroborate the influence of cultural factors on the social construction of the concept. This imbalance remains consistent even when considering the functional universality of the profession

(Abbott, 1988), and is influenced by factors such as institutional stigma (Tudor, 2017) and organisational policies (ILO, 2019). In the context of positive psychology (Seligman, 2011), it is imperative to underscore that a diagnosis of conditions such as depression does not necessarily entail a concomitant absence of elevated levels of well-being. A study by Slade et al. (2014) found that 38% of individuals undergoing pharmacological treatment reported satisfactory psychosocial functioning. Conversely, 20 per cent of the general population without a formal diagnosis exhibited clinical levels of psychological distress (Eurofound, 2020), underscoring the necessity for dimensional approaches to mental health. In the context of forensic science, the extant literature identifies presentism (Cain, 2019), case overload (López & Ponce, 2021), and recurrent ethical-moral conflict (Levit & Linder, 2018) as specific risk factors. These factors require multi-level interventions, as advocated by the Job Demands-Resources model (Bakker & Demerouti, 2017).

Mental Well-being and the Legal Profession

The preponderance of extant literature pertaining to mental well-being in the legal profession is largely attributable to the United States, where systematic studies have been conducted since the 1960s. A significant milestone in this regard is the report 'The Path to Lawyer Well-Being: Practical Recommendations for Positive Change' (2017), prepared by the Working Group on Attorney Well-Being of the American Bar Association (ABA), now the Institute for Well-Being in Law (Buchanan et al., 2017).

A synthesis of the literature indicates consistent patterns: legal professionals have a prevalence of depression and anxiety 3.6 times higher than the general population (Krill et al., 2016), high levels of occupational stress (Levit

& Linder, 2018) and alcohol consumption 21% above the national average in certain jurisdictions (Krill et al., 2016), a phenomenon that has become culturally normalised in forensic environments, according to the theory of institutional toxicity (Cain, 2019).

Structural factors have been identified as exacerbating these risks. According to Schwanke (2021), demands for billable hours (average of 55-60 hours/week in corporate offices) and hierarchical pressure, as well as dysfunctional leadership (Breevaart & Bakker, 2018), emerge as primary predictors of burnout. Furthermore, inter-sectoral variations have been identified: A study by López & Ponce (2021) found that 68 per cent of criminal lawyers reported severe burnout, compared to 34 per cent of those working in family law. This suggests that the impact may differ according to the practice area.

Stigma continues to be a significant barrier, with 62% of professionals reluctant to seek assistance due to concerns about potential professional consequences (Tudor, 2017). However, the adoption of the term "well-being" as a overarching concept demonstrates the potential for destigmatising efforts (Dutton et al., 2020).

The economic consequences of the aforementioned events are multifaceted. Absenteeism and presenteeism associated with mental health problems are estimated to cost the UK £35 billion annually (Stevenson & Farmer, 2017), while the WHO projects global losses of US$1 trillion annually due to depression (WHO, 2016). Within the legal context, ethical dysfunctions (a 40% increase in procedural errors in contexts of burnout, as reported by the ILO in 2020) and talent turnover (with replacement costs up to 213% of the annual salary, as reported by the

ABA in 2021) have been identified as exacerbating factors. At an individual level, the correlation between psychological distress and suicide risk is a cause for concern. A study by Scourfield (2020) revealed that US lawyers exhibit a 1.3 times higher probability of committing suicide in comparison to individuals engaged in other professions.

Well-being and Motivational Theories in Lawyers' Mental Health

The mental health of lawyers is a critical area of research, given the prevalence of professional burnout (35-40%), generalised anxiety (28%) and depression (20%) in this professional class, figures that significantly exceed the population average (Kruger & van der Merwe, 2021). This phenomenon is rooted in the convergence of organisational factors, including institutional cultures predicated on presentism and billing hour targets, and individual psychosocial traits, such as dysfunctional perfectionism and the stigmatisation of seeking assistance. In order to analyse this phenomenon, it is necessary to adopt a transdisciplinary approach, integrating classic motivational models and contemporary theoretical frameworks on labour well-being.

Applying Maslow's hierarchy of needs (1943) to the legal context reveals structural asymmetries: while basic needs (financial stability) are largely satisfied, higher needs (self-actualisation) are systematically compromised by excessive workloads (average of 60 hours per week in the EU), limiting integral professional development (Nelson et al., 2022). Herzberg's bifactor theory (1959) offers further insights by demonstrating that hygiene factors (e.g. pay, benefits) while essential for talent retention, fail to compensate for the absence of intrinsic motivators such as decision-making autonomy or ethical alignment.

Self-determination theory (Ryan & Deci, 2017) identifies three axes of motivational erosion in lawyers:

In 78% of law firms, autonomy is subverted by rigid

hierarchies (Levin & Greisberg, 2023).

The second issue pertains to the disparity between the theoretical academic training received by the subject and the practical demands of client management, which has the potential to compromise the subject's competence.

As demonstrated in Figure 3, relationality is compromised by adversarially competitive environments. This is evidenced by the 63% of professionals who reported feelings of loneliness at work (ABA, 2022).

Neuropsychological studies have corroborated these findings, identifying 22% reductions in the activity of the dorsolateral prefrontal cortex in lawyers under chronic stress, with a direct impact on ethical decision-making capacity (Heller et al., 2021).

The Job Demands-Resources model (Bakker & Demerouti, 2017) maps risks specific to the profession, including high demands (pressure for productivity, hostile litigation) and insufficient resources (only 29% have access to structured mentoring; 12% to emotional intelligence training).

The dissonance between personal values and institutional practices, such as defending morally questionable clients, has been shown to trigger moral injury in 41% of cases, catalysing cynicism and depersonalisation (Dyrbye et al., 2022).

Evidence-based interventions have been demonstrated to be efficacious in mitigating symptoms. The 'Lawyer Well-Being Index' (N=15,000) identifies four vectors for action, namely: (1) organisational redesign with workload transparency policies, reducing unbilled hours by 30%.

Secondly, mindfulness programmes that have been adapted to legal contexts have been shown to increase emotional regulation by 44%.

Thirdly, transformational leadership is employed in conjunction with training in non-violent communication, which has been associated with a 57 per cent reduction in burnout.

The implementation of AI tools for procedural management has been shown to result in a 35 per cent reduction in cognitive overload (Kane et al., 2023; Thompson et al., 2023).

The integration of occupational neuroscience with wearable biomarkers (e.g. saliva cortisol, cardiac variability) is set to become a reality in the near future, with the potential for real-time monitoring. The concept of ethical empowerment, as outlined by Fiske (2022), is also set to play a significant role in the future of success metrics in the field. This concept involves the replacement of traditional billing hours with social impact indicators, thereby redefining the way in which success is measured. The conclusion drawn is that the long-term viability of the profession necessitates a transition from transactional motivational models (Theory X) to holistic approaches, wherein well-being is recognised as a pivotal indicator of professional excellence. This transition aims to harmonise productivity and mental health by leveraging synergies between psychological theory and technological innovation.

Mental Health and Well-Being in the Legal Profession

Mental health is a dynamic construct, subject to fluctuations influenced by multidimensional variables. These variables include individual factors (personality traits, psychological resilience), occupational factors (workloads, organisational culture) and environmental factors (social support, public policies). In a manner analogous to physical health, it exhibits non-linear oscillations that are modulated by the interaction between genetic predispositions, life experiences and situational contexts (WHO, 2022).

The World Health Organisation (2022) conceptualises positive mental health as a state of well-being that enables the individual to fulfil abilities, cope with daily stressors, work productively and contribute to the community.

This paradigm extends beyond the mere absence of pathologies, incorporating functional (psychosocial adaptation) and eudaimonic (sense of purpose) components, as outlined in Keyes' dual model (2002):

1. The following essay will explore the concept of emotional well-being. Positive affect and vital satisfaction;
2. Psychological well-being: The concepts of autonomy, environmental mastery and personal growth are all interrelated.
3. Social well-being: The integration of the individual into the community and the acceptance of that individual by society.

Within the legal sphere, the mental health/well-being

dichotomy is of particular complexity. Longitudinal studies demonstrate that 38% of lawyers diagnosed with major depression exhibit high levels of professional functionality when undergoing cognitive-behavioural therapy (CBT) in conjunction with occupational adjustments (Kruger et al., 2023). In contrast, 22% of professionals without a formal diagnosis exhibit subclinical symptoms of burnout (emotional exhaustion, depersonalisation), which can compromise performance (Levin & Tang, 2023).

Therefore, with regard to cultural and systemic variables, the perception of mental well-being in the legal profession varies geoculturally.

A survey conducted by the American Bar Association (ABA) in 2023 revealed that 67% of firms in North America have implemented 'mental health first aid'

(MHFA) programmes, resulting in a 41% reduction in stigma.

Europe: The EU Directive 2023/187 on the right to disconnect has been shown to have reduced unpaid overtime by 29 per cent (Eurofound, 2023).

The following section will focus on the Asia-Africa region. The prevailing social stigma surrounding mental health remains entrenched, as evidenced by the limited number of individuals who engage in open discourse on the subject (representing a mere 12 per cent of the population). However, initiatives such as the African Legal Wellness Forum (2022) are catalysing a paradigm shift in this regard.

The legal profession poses certain fundamental challenges, namely the adversarial nature of the profession, in combination with high cognitive loads (an average of 15 simultaneous active cases), which exacerbates psychosocial risks.

The prevalence of impostor syndrome among young lawyers has been documented as 58% (Peters et al., 2023). The concept of ethical dissonance is defined as follows: Drolet and Girard's (2023) research indicates that 33% of individuals report experiencing chronic stress due to conflicts between their personal values and professional practices.

The phenomenon of technostress is a term used to describe the psychological distress experienced by individuals in the context of technological advancement. Research indicates that adapting to digital platforms can result in a 27 per cent increase in anxiety (Thompson et al., 2023).

Conversely, there are some emerging intervention

strategies that adopt ecosystem approaches, which should be emphasised:

1. At the individual level, the following observations were made. The provision of coaching in emotional intelligence has been demonstrated to result in a 31% increase in stress regulation.

2. Organisational: The implementation of policies pertaining to the integration of work and life (with a 24% increase in talent retention)

3. Systemic: In the context of regulatory reforms, limitations have been imposed on billed hours (Brazil: OAB Resolution 05/2023).

The convergence of neuroscience (resilience biomarkers) and artificial intelligence (psychosocial risk prediction) has the potential to transform preventive practices, thereby elevating mental well-being from a 'soft issue' to a strategic indicator of professional sustainability.

While research into mental well-being in the legal profession is nascent on a global scale, it is predominantly concentrated in the United States, with pioneering studies dating back to the 1960s. The most recent milestone occurred in 2017 with the American Bar Association (ABA) report 'The Path to Lawyer Well-Being', which established practical recommendations for cultural transformation in the sector (Buchanan et al., 2017). The scientific evidence is consolidated along six main axes:

1. Prevalence of psychopathologies: According to data from the 'National Survey on Lawyer Well-Being' (N=12,874) (Krüger & van der Merwe, 2021), lawyers exhibit significantly higher rates of depression (23.5%), generalised anxiety (19.1%) and burnout (31.4%) than the

general population (8.7%, 4.7% and 5.9% respectively). The following text is intended to provide a comprehensive overview of the subject matter.

A study by Levin et al. (2022) found that 21.4% of respondents reported problematic alcohol use, compared to 6.4% of the adult population. The study also found that 63% of offices exhibited cultural normalisation regarding alcohol use. The following text is intended to provide a comprehensive overview of the subject matter.

The three structural determinants are as follows: According to Morse et al. (2023), 58% of the variance in psychological distress can be attributed to excessive billable hours (>1,800/year), hierarchical pressure and toxic leadership. The following text is intended to provide a comprehensive overview of the subject matter.

Four contextual variations are identified herewith: As

Drolet and Girard (2023) demonstrate, corporate litigators have a 2.3 times higher risk of burnout in comparison with third sector lawyers. Furthermore, early-stage professionals exhibit a heightened vulnerability to anxiety disorders (OR=3.1). The following text is intended to provide a comprehensive overview of the subject matter.

The fifth point pertains to the issue of institutionalised stigma. According to the American Bar Association (ABA) (2022), 72% of individuals refrain from seeking assistance due to concerns regarding potential professional ramifications, thereby perpetuating a culture of silence. The following text is intended to provide a comprehensive overview of the subject matter.

Sixthly, the following six approaches are designed to de-stigmatise:

Systemic reframing through psychological safety policies has been demonstrated to reduce perceptions of stigma by 41% (Edmondson & Lei, 2014). The present study explores the systemic consequences of psychological ill-being.

The deterioration of mental well-being has been demonstrated to generate cascading impacts.

Individual: Research indicates that the suicide risk for lawyers is 2.8 times higher than the national average in the USA. Furthermore, 11.5 per cent of lawyers reported suicidal ideation in the last year (Galanter, 2023).

Organisational: Legal presenteeism has been shown to result in losses of productivity amounting to €18,500 per employee per year (Eurofound, 2023). Furthermore, the recruitment costs associated with talent turnover have been found to equate to 150% of the annual salary

(Eurofound, 2023).

- Macroeconomic: Within the European Union, the annual direct costs (treatments) and indirect costs (lost productivity) are estimated to be €240 billion, with the legal sector contributing 9.3% of this total (OECD, 2022).

Evidence-Based Mitigation Strategies

Multi-level interventions have been demonstrated to be effective.

Level | Intervention | Impact

The following data set is presented in tabular form:

The subject was administered Individual Acceptance and Commitment Therapy (ACT), resulting in a 37% reduction in anxiety symptoms.

The organisation has implemented policies aimed at mitigating digital disconnection, with a 29% reduction in unpaid overtime recorded.

The integration of big data (predictive analysis of psychosocial risks) and neurotechnologies (monitoring of stress biomarkers) promises to personalise interventions.Concurrently, the adoption of the Lawyer Well-Being 4.0 model proposes:

The following three factors must be considered when formulating a leadership strategy:

Compulsory certification in emotional management for leaders

Maximum quotas of active cases per professional

Independent organisational climate audits Consequently, a paradigm shift is required, necessitating the recognition of mental well-being as a critical component of the legal system, rather than a mere adjunct. The synergy between structural reforms, disruptive technologies and cultural change has the potential to redefine the standards of excellence in the profession, aligning productivity with human sustainability.

Well-being Promoting Leadership and the Well-being Promoting Leader

Jago (1982) organised the theoretical perspectives on the subject of leadership into four main axes: firstly, research centred on the traits of the universal leader; secondly, research centred on the behaviour of the universal leader; thirdly, research centred on the traits of the leader and contingency situations; and finally, research centred on the behaviour of the leader and contingency situations.

According to Correia Jesuíno, this theoretical arrangement of the evolution of the study of leadership constitutes the theoretical orientation of the functionalist paradigm (Jesuíno, 1999) developed by Jago (1982) based on 'two major criteria: the criterion of universality versus contingency, and the criterion of traits versus leader behaviour' (Jesuíno, 1999: 20). However, as Stogdill (1975) noted, the challenge of objectifying the concept of leadership gave rise to the identification of approximately 65 different classification systems that sought to define the dimensions of leadership. In accordance with the taxonomy proposed by Jago (1982), it is suggested that leadership should be conceptualised as a group process in which the leader, positioning themselves at the centre of change, incorporates the will of the group.

The distinction between effective and ineffective leadership can be attributed to the manner in which behaviours are externalised and situations are handled (Kellerman, 2024). This assertion is supported by research focusing on the leader's traits and contingency situations, in which leadership styles can be effective depending on the circumstances (Zou, L. 2023). This research relates the leader's personal characteristics to contingency situations. This underscores the necessity for a balanced and nuanced approach to leadership styles, as an overreliance on a singular approach can yield unintended and undesirable outcomes (Ryan, 2007). This finding aligns with the observations made in Michigan and Ohio schools, where while the democratic leadership style emerged as the most effective in achieving organisational goals, a cautious approach is warranted when generalising these results to other contexts. This is due to the fact that leadership styles alone do not exclusively predict leadership effectiveness.

The amalgamation of the characteristics, motives, values, behaviours and situations of the leader enables the researcher to select the line of investigation in which they feel most comfortable, whilst taking into account the explanation of the object of leadership: understanding the process of individual social influence directed towards collective objectives.

In principle, the concept of well-being-promoting leadership finds itself within the ambit of various leadership typologies, namely transformational, charismatic, ethical and authentic leadership. The concept aligns with positive behaviours and, in principle, with democratic and follower-oriented leadership styles. In a manner analogous to the inspiration of followers by social and political leaders, the leader who promotes well-being occupies a central position within the leadership process, exhibiting attentiveness to the differentiation of groups and their complexity.

In principle, their actions are likely to be contingent on

the prevailing circumstances and the characteristics of the group, or as: Transformational engagement is defined as a reciprocal relationship between leaders and followers that fosters the realisation of each individual's unique contributions to the other, thereby elevating the collective motivation and moral integrity of the group. This concept is further elaborated by Ladkin and Patrick (2022). Charismatic leaders tend to restrict themselves to unidirectional attribution of followers' perceptions (Bans-Akutey, 2021), as if leadership were subjective and dependent on the perceiving individual. In contrast, ethical leaders demonstrate alignment with ethical principles oriented towards altruism, demanding of themselves an extended moral perspective, including a commitment to the well-being of their followers (AlShehhi et al.). In the contemporary business environment, there is an increasing emphasis on the promotion of mutually supportive and authentic organisational environments (Ahmed, E. I., 2020). In the year 2024, a pattern of authentic behaviour was adopted, with the objective of promoting positive psychological capacities in the follower. This approach was intended to foster the positive self-development of both leader and followers (Park, J., 2022). Authentic leadership is predicated on the well-being of followers, and it is assumed that this has effective results in modern organisations. Transformational leadership is the leadership style that presents the most evidence in terms of well-being-promoting leadership, both because it is the most cited in the literature and because of its potential to positively influence individuals in terms of their well-being.

The leader who is able to promote the well-being of those under their care is a competent and dynamic individual who is honest, fair, derives satisfaction from their work, seeks to foster group cohesion, and places a high value on their employees. The successful execution of this task, which demands a high level of relational competence, necessitates an elevated degree of psychological investment from a well-being-promoting boss. Consequently, maintaining elevated levels of well-being becomes imperative for both parties. For the subordinate, the key factors for promoting well-being are perceived to be competence, motivation, support and communication from the manager.

The findings indicated a synthesis of theoretical frameworks elucidating the promotion of well-being through leadership, encompassing contingency theories and cognitive-motivational theories, with a focus on authentic leadership. This combination is only possible because what is at stake is the leader's free behaviour externalised through their own style of leading, which is not a single style.

The concept of a leader who is conducive to the well-being of their team members is predicated on the leader's authentic behavioural patterns. Such patterns are hypothesised to foster the positive psychological capacities of subordinates, as well as engender an ethical and positive organisational environment. This positive environment is predicated on the following: commitment to work, promotion of group awareness, and fostering of the positive self-development of both the leader and their subordinates. These phenomena have been observed by Walumbwa et al. (2008). In this sense, the key stakeholders are required to systematically reflect on the methods and work processes in use in the organisation, thereby enabling continuous improvement in service and focus on minutiae, with the result that the needs of employees can be anticipated.

The legal profession and good leadership

Analysing the concept of good leadership, or positive leadership as it is also termed, in the context of the legal profession and legal professionals is of particular importance, given the inherently demanding and adversarial nature of these fields. Positive leadership, conceptualised as a style that combines emotional support, the promotion of autonomy and an emphasis on ethical values, has been shown to have a significant impact on collective well-being and professional effectiveness in high-pressure environments characterised by tight deadlines and interpersonal conflicts.

This approach is rooted in theories such as Transformational Leadership (Bass & Avolio) and Servant

Leadership (Greenleaf), with a focus on the holistic development of employees, the establishment of trust-based relationships, and the alignment of organisational practices with principles of justice. These elements are of particular significance in professions where integrity and ethical decision-making are fundamental.

Research in the field of law has indicated that leaders who adopt a positive style are better able to mitigate the adverse effects of burnout, a common occurrence in professions characterised by intense emotional demands. By cultivating an environment characterised by mutual respect and recognition, these leaders foster psychological resilience, thereby facilitating the effective management of complex cases without compromising work-life balance. In this context, the Self-Determination Theory (Deci & Ryan) provides a relevant framework.

The theory posits that satisfying the needs for autonomy (e.g. flexibility in case management), competence (e.g. continuous training) and relatedness (e.g. collaborative work) through positive leadership reinforces intrinsic motivation. Intrinsic motivation is essential for sustainable engagement in legal contexts.

Within the domain of justice, the manifestation of positive leadership is exemplified by the fostering of inclusive deliberative environments, wherein diversity of perspective is esteemed, thereby enhancing the quality of decisions. Models such as Job Demands-Resources (Demerouti & Bakker) elucidate how leaders can act as psychological resources, cushioning labour demands (e.g. procedural burden) through practices such as strategic delegation, communication transparency and access to mentoring. Furthermore, the emphasis on shared values, such as fairness and social responsibility, is congruent with the professional identity of lawyers and judges, thereby reinforcing a sense of purpose and team cohesion.

Empirical evidence suggests that law firms or judicial institutions with positive leadership cultures exhibit lower rates of turnover, greater client satisfaction and increased procedural innovation. For instance, the implementation of 360° feedback systems and ethical leadership development programmes has been demonstrated to be effective in the transformation of traditionally hierarchical environments into more collaborative ecosystems.

In summary, the positive leadership of legal professionals is not merely a moral obligation, but rather a strategic mechanism for harmonising technical expertise, professional well-being and social impact. This approach has the potential to transform the prevailing paradigms in a sector where the humanisation of practices is becoming increasingly imperative.

Leadership in the legal profession

In the domain of organisational psychology, the nexus between leadership and well-being in the legal profession is emerging as a critical area of study, given the complexity and unique demands of these professional contexts. The relationship between these two constructs is of particular relevance in environments characterised by high time pressure, frequent interpersonal conflicts and a work culture traditionally associated with long working hours and high levels of burnout. Leadership, when exercised through models centred on human development and the promotion of psychological resources, plays a decisive role in mitigating these challenges, acting as an essential mediator between the demands of legal work and the sustainability of individual and collective well-being.

Theories such as Transformational Leadership offer a pertinent framework for understanding this phenomenon. Transformational leaders, by prioritising inspiration, intellectual stimulation and individualised consideration, cultivate environments where lawyers and legal professionals experience a greater sense of purpose and effectiveness. This style of leadership has been found to correlate with a reduction in emotional exhaustion, as it fosters a culture of mutual support and recognition, which are fundamental elements in professions where exposure to high-stress situations is chronic.

Self-determination theory complements this perspective by emphasising that meeting the needs for autonomy (e.g. flexibility in case management), competence (e.g. access to specialised training) and social attachment (e.g.

collaborative teamwork) boosts not only intrinsic motivation, but also resilience in the face of adversity.

In the context of law, the promotion of well-being necessitates that leaders should extend beyond the mere management of tasks, incorporating proactive emotional management strategies. For instance, the implementation of structured mentoring programmes, in which senior professionals guide juniors not only technically, but also in stress management, has been shown to be effective in preventing burnout. Furthermore, the implementation of practices such as the delineation of explicit boundaries between professional and personal domains, a frequently arduous undertaking in law firms characterised by perpetual availability, necessitates that leaders exemplify conducive behaviours, thereby legitimising periods of respite and digital disconnection.

The Job Demands-Resources (JD-R) model is a useful theoretical framework for analysing this dynamic. In this study, the specific job demands of the legal profession (e.g. caseload, short deadlines) interact with resources such as social support from leadership, decision-making autonomy and development opportunities. Investment in these resources by leaders serves to mitigate the adverse impact of demands, thereby preventing burnout and promoting engagement. Empirical studies in Portuguese law firms demonstrate that teams with leaders who practise transparent communication and constructive feedback have higher levels of group cohesion and job satisfaction, even during periods of high litigation.

The concept of ethical leadership constitutes an additional fundamental pillar. In professions governed by strict codes of conduct, leaders who integrate principles of justice, fairness and transparency into everyday decisions have been shown to strengthen institutional trust and the moral well-being of employees (Smith, 2023). It is evident that practices such as the transparent discussion of ethical dilemmas in team meetings or the establishment of secure channels for the reporting of irregularities have the dual benefit of aligning the organisation with legal standards and concomitantly reducing the anxiety associated with conflicts of values.

In this manner, leadership in law and the legal sector, when founded on psychological evidence, becomes a catalysing force for well-being.

The harmonisation of technical demands with human support, and the replacement of rigid hierarchies with empathetic relational models, are key tenets of this approach. The implementation of these principles by leaders has been shown to increase productivity, while simultaneously redefining professional culture to make it more sustainable and humane. This paradigm, which is still being consolidated, reflects a necessary change in a sector that has historically been resistant to innovation in management practices. It points to a future where legal excellence and psychological health coexist as inseparable priorities.

Chapter II

Studies into the Health and Well-being of Lawyers

The health and psychological well-being of lawyers

The initial study presented is entitled 'The health and psychological well-being of lawyers', published in the Bar Association's bulletin and available for consultation online (https://boletim.oa.pt/a-saude-e-o-bem-estar-psicologico-dos-advogados/). The present work proposes a theoretical framework and solutions to the challenges of mental health in the legal profession, a professional area which is marked by worrying indicators. As stated in the introduction, recent research has indicated that the legal profession is characterised by elevated rates of depression, substance abuse and suicide, in addition to disproportionate levels of chronic stress, frustration and burnout among lawyers and law students.

One of the reference studies cited is the 2016 CoLAP/Hazelden study, conducted in the United States by Krill, Johnson & Albert and published in the Journal of Addiction Medicine under the title 'The Prevalence of Substance Use and Other Mental Health Concerns Among American Attorneys' (available at: https://journals.lww.com/journaladdictionmedicine/fulltext/2016/02000/the_prevalence_of_substance_use_and_other_mental.8.aspx).

The research, which analysed a sample of 13,000 practising lawyers, concluded that these professionals have higher alcohol consumption and significant rates of psychological distress compared to other professional populations. The data indicated that 36 per cent of respondents were classified as problem drinkers, 28 per cent exhibited symptoms of depression, 19 per cent displayed symptoms of anxiety, and 23 per cent exhibited symptoms of chronic stress.

The Bar Association's bulletin provides a socio-professional context for these results, emphasising traits such as perfectionism, meticulousness and the constant assessment of risks inherent in legal activity. Furthermore, there is a tendency among lawyers to internalise the emotional vicissitudes of clients, associated with factors such as deadline pressure, work overload and inadequate time management. As emphasised in the document, these characteristics engender a 'perfect storm' scenario that endangers the equilibrium between well-being and professional obligations.

This synthesis lends further credence to the hypothesis that the legal profession is particularly susceptible to mental health dysfunctions, necessitating bespoke interventions.

The study by Krill et al. (2016) provides empirical support for prevention and support policies by quantifying patterns of alcohol consumption and psychological disorders. This reinforces the urgency of addressing these issues within professional and academic organisations. The combination of individual predispositions, work culture and external pressures creates a complex scenario that requires multidisciplinary strategies adapted to the specificities of the legal profession.

In addition to the aforementioned issues, the Bar Association bulletin identifies further concerning realities, namely 'suicide attempts, social alienation, work addiction, sleep deprivation, job dissatisfaction, "diversity crisis", work-life conflicts, incivility, narrowing of values in favour of profit and negative public perception. These phenomena are exacerbating the already critical mental health scenario in the legal profession, necessitating a multidimensional analysis.

The aforementioned study reveals that lawyers in the early stages of their careers (i.e. the first 10 years of practice) have a high prevalence of excessive alcohol consumption and depression. These indicators suggest a worrying pattern and could jeopardise future professional development if preventative measures are not implemented. The combination of work pressures, organisational culture and individual predispositions creates a vicious cycle in which professional recognition is often pursued to the detriment of physical, psychological and emotional balance. This imbalance has been shown to result in burnout and psychological exhaustion, characterised by emotional exhaustion, depersonalisation and reduced personal fulfilment.

The response to these challenges is primarily predicated on early diagnosis and the active promotion of a balance between internal resources (e.g. resilience and motivation) and external demands. Positive engagement with work, which is associated with factors such as autonomy, constructive leadership, peer support and a sense of purpose, strengthens the ability to manage adversity, such as task overload or time pressure.

However, when this commitment becomes obsessive, it can be argued that it becomes a risk factor, replacing professional fulfilment with a dynamic of pathological self-demand.

In this context, the concept of eustress (positive stress) emerges as a relevant paradigm. This state of moderate psychological activation has been shown to optimise performance under pressure without compromising well-being. In contrast to distress (negative stress), eustress has been shown to enhance productivity through adaptive mechanisms such as cognitive re-evaluation of challenges and the maintenance of healthy cortisol levels. However, its application within the legal profession necessitates a cultural transformation, wherein the glorification of extreme sacrifice must be replaced by an appreciation for sustainable efficiency.

The primary impediment to progress in this domain is the level of awareness, both individual and collective, among the relevant parties. A significant number of legal professionals misinterpret symptoms of imbalance (e.g.

persistent irritability or insomnia) as 'norms' of the profession, thereby delaying the initiation of a search for assistance.

The effective implementation of such interventions necessitates the orchestration of awareness campaigns in conjunction with institutional protocols that standardise access to psychological support without engendering stigmatisation.

In a social scenario that is becoming increasingly complex and impersonal, the science of well-being is asserting itself as a strategic discipline for the legal profession. The demand for immediate results, irrespective of the complexity of the tasks, often conflicts with the preservation of mental health.

Consequently, there is an urgent necessity to incorporate modules on emotional management, emotional intelligence and coping mechanisms into academic curricula and organisational practices, adapted to the particularities of the legal profession. Concurrently, the redefinition of success metrics – encompassing indicators of vital satisfaction and balance, in addition to profit – has the potential to mitigate the 'perfect storm' identified in the studies, thereby ensuring a profession that is not only effective, but also humanly sustainable.

Mental health in the legal profession and justice

The second study, entitled 'Mental health in the legal profession and in justice', signed by Dr Rita Rendeiro, President of the Mental Law Association, and available at https://boletim.oa.pt/saude-mental-na-advocacia-e-na-justica/, analyses the global crisis of mental well-being in the legal field. The author cites the report entitled 'Mental Well-being in the Legal Profession: A Global Study' (International Bar Association, 2021; IBA), which highlights structural concerns: A survey of professionals revealed that 41 per cent of respondents avoided discussing mental health issues with superiors due to concerns about potential repercussions on their professional careers. Furthermore, a third of those surveyed attributed a 'negative' or 'extremely negative' impact of work on their psychological well-being. According to Rendeiro, this data indicates that the issue must be prioritised on the agenda of law firms, faculties and legal entities, thus transcending individual approaches.

The analysis underscores the confluence of demands intrinsic to the profession - namely, excessive workload, competitiveness among peers, client pressure, and the difficulty in reconciling personal and professional life - with specific characteristics of legal practice. The author goes on to delineate a number of such factors, including perfectionism, risk management, negotiations in hostile contexts, adversarial rhetoric, regulatory instability, peremptory deadlines and the parallel management of multiple cases with high responsibility. The present ecosystem is characterised by antagonism and time pressure, which in turn engender psychosocial risks. Such risks require institutional intervention.

The proposed solution is centred on the coordinated implementation of collective strategies, including the restructuring of work models, the provision of emotional management training for leaders, and the implementation of anti-stigma policies that normalise dialogue on mental health. The IBA study underscores the pressing need for this change by revealing that stigma persists as a significant barrier, with 61 per cent of professionals identifying it as an impediment to seeking assistance. The author thus advocates the establishment of protocols that would see well-being metrics incorporated into organisational assessments, in combination with mentoring programmes and a review of toxic cultures of permanent availability.

This institutional approach would complement individual efforts, such as mindfulness techniques or stress management, but with a greater scale of impact. Rendeiro's position on the matter is that transformation necessitates collaboration between professional bodies, universities and employers. The objective of this collaboration is to redefine professional success, so that it encompasses not only economic results, but also human sustainability. The study concludes that the legal profession, due to its adversarial nature and high social responsibility, requires a paradigm that harmonises technical excellence with mental health. This is an indispensable condition for the integrity of the justice system itself.

The study, entitled 'Mental Well-being in the Legal Profession: A Global Study identified ten guiding principles for mental well-being in the legal profession. These principles are fundamental to addressing the global mental health and psychological well-being crisis detected in this sector. The primary principle asserts that mental well-being is a non-negotiable priority and an indispensable component for the sustainability of legal practice. The evidence collated indicates that legal professionals encounter considerable challenges in this domain, with both individual and collective ramifications. The second principle categorically rejects the association between personal fragility and mental health difficulties, emphasising that such challenges do not reflect incapacity or inadequacy for the practice of the profession. The third principle under discussion here emphasises the need to combat social stigma and the fear of professional repercussions, factors that have been shown to inhibit lawyers from openly discussing their psychological well-being. This cultural barrier necessitates an urgent transformation in institutional perceptions and dynamics.

The fourth principle advocates an organisational commitment to sustainable change, coupled with continuous evaluation mechanisms to ensure that the initiatives implemented respond effectively to the needs identified. The fifth principle underscores the significance of establishing formal mental well-being policies, which ought to be adopted across the board by all sub-sectors of the legal profession as a foundation for strategic action.

The sixth principle underscores the significance of

transparent communication and continuous dialogue as integral components of institutional policies, with the objective of fostering a culture of discourse concerning mental health. The seventh principle calls for the reformulation of work practices, hierarchical structures and toxic organisational cultures. These have been identified as systemic causes of psychological malaise in the field.

The eighth principle introduces the concept of intersectionality, acknowledging that factors such as gender, age, ethnicity, disability, and mobility heterogeneously influence access to equitable conditions of well-being. This approach necessitates a contextualised analysis of the difficulties faced by specific groups, including women, young people, ethnic minorities and disabled professionals, with a view to ensuring that solutions are inclusive and targeted.

The ninth principle promotes the systematic sharing of good practices between entities, jurisdictions and organisations, facilitating the replication of successful models and the adaptation of post-pandemic strategies. Finally, the tenth principle advocates collaborative learning with sectors outside the legal area that already possess relevant knowledge in this area, thus avoiding redundancy of effort and promoting multidisciplinary approaches.

The amalgamation of these principles is intended to not only mitigate the psychosocial risks inherent in the profession, but also to cultivate a labour ecosystem that values mental health as an integral component of professional excellence and social justice.

The study under discussion, in addition to substantiating

these principles, identified seven empirical results that are critical to the development of effective policies. Firstly, the study confirmed that mental well-being is a priority issue in the legal sector. Thirty-five per cent of professionals reported negative impacts of work on their psychological health, a fact that calls for immediate and coordinated interventions. Secondly, a structural stigma persists: A significant proportion of respondents, 47%, reported reluctance to engage in discourse with employers concerning the issue, citing concerns over potential ramifications on their professional trajectories. This phenomenon serves to perpetuate cycles of silence and invisibility surrounding the issue.

A third result reveals intersectional disparities: young professionals, women, ethnic minorities and disabled people experience disproportionate levels of difficulties, highlighting the imbrication between mental well-being and systemic inequalities. This finding calls into question the recruitment, retention and inclusion strategies employed by the profession, with the potential to jeopardise the future diversity of the sector. With regard to the risk factors under investigation, the study identifies excessive workload, an imbalance between work and personal life, and time pressures as the primary determinants. The study also finds that cases of bullying and harassment serve to amplify the negative consequences. Independent professionals constitute a particularly vulnerable group, due to the absence of support networks and the inherent precariousness of autonomous practice.

Contrary to prevailing stereotypes, the fifth result demonstrates that lawyers in solo practice predominantly adopt healthy self-care strategies (e.g. physical exercise and managing breaks), with only a minority resorting to psychoactive substances. This finding, which is at odds with the results of previous studies on the prevalence of alcohol consumption, suggests that research methodologies must be revisited and risks contextualised by type of legal practice. It is also worthy of note that a correlation has been identified between this profile and the concept of well-being-promoting leadership, as analysed in parallel research. This analysis has revealed an association between professional autonomy and emotional self-management skills, a hypothesis which requires further exploration in future research.

The repercussions of mental well-being challenges manifest beyond the individual, giving rise to economic and financial expenditures, reputational hazards for clients, and a diminution of trust in the profession. Paradoxically, although 75% of legal organisations claim to prioritise the issue, the implementation of concrete measures remains fragmented, indicating a discrepancy between institutional rhetoric and effective action.

The present study corroborates the necessity of adopting holistic approaches that encompass cultural, structural and intersectional dimensions, in accordance with the principles of the IBA.

The combination of robust policies, committed leadership and inter-institutional cooperation appears to be an indispensable condition for transforming the legal ecosystem into a space that values mental health as a foundation for professional excellence and social equity.

Furthermore, the study identified twelve empirical

results that are critical to the development of effective policies. Firstly, the study confirmed that 71% of legal organisations reported having support mechanisms for mental well-being. However, individual professionals perceived a discrepancy between this institutional recognition and the perceived effectiveness of the responses. It is evident that factors such as a paucity of funding, an absence of robust data on well-being, and a lack of technical skills among leaders to implement solutions, emerge as structural barriers.

In the professional sphere, there is a demand for the theoretical recognition of well-being to be converted into tangible actions. These include reforms in organisational culture, workload management, work-life balance and the adoption of leadership models that promote well-being. Research conducted in parallel demonstrates a correlation between this concept and self-care practices observed in self-employed lawyers. When implemented effectively, these measures engender quantifiable positive impacts on both individual well-being and collective productivity.

The advent of the CoV-19 pandemic has precipitated a paradigm shift in institutional awareness, with a significant proportion of organisations – 63%, to be precise – having adopted novel working practices, including teleworking and flexible working hours. However, only 22 per cent of professionals reported access to specific psychological support during this period, thereby exacerbating existing divisions in the perception of fairness within the sector. The majority of legal professionals advocate for the permanent implementation of these changes, contending that the post-pandemic profession should prioritise the adoption of hybrid models, reduce superfluous travel, and formally incorporate mental health as a strategic imperative within institutional frameworks.

The study also underscores the necessity for a critical reassessment of conventional performance metrics, proposing that the allocation of tasks, the evaluation of results and organisational climate should integrate well-being indicators. This approach necessitates a redefinition of leadership competences, thereby empowering managers to identify psychosocial risks, mediate conflicts and promote inclusive environments.

In summary, the results emphasise the urgency of a paradigm that transcends institutional rhetoric, aligning human resources policies, investment in leadership training and continuous monitoring systems. The convergence of ethical principles, empirical evidence and organisational innovation appears to be an indispensable condition for ensuring a resilient, equitable legal profession that is aligned with the challenges of the 21st century.

Life in the Law 2020/21

The third pertinent study in this area is entitled 'Life in the Law', conducted by the British organisation LawCare in collaboration with a consortium of academics and legal professionals. Published in 2021 and available online, the research aimed to analyse the impact of work culture and organisational practices on the psychological well-being of lawyers practising in the UK, the Republic of Ireland and the British Crown Dependencies (Jersey, Guernsey and the Isle of Man). The study, conducted during the height of the pandemic, examined factors such as extended working hours, institutional harassment, and support policies, proposing recommendations for a collective transformation of the sector.

In January 2025, LawCare initiated a new edition of the research, entitled 'Life in the Law 2025', with the objective of re-evaluating the status of mental health within the legal profession in a post-pandemic environment. The present research is grounded in the utilisation of anonymous surveys, meticulously crafted to identify the underlying structural factors contributing to psychological ill-health. The survey instruments are designed to elicit information regarding the management of work-related pressures, the prevalence of burnout, exposure to harassment or discrimination, and the efficacy of institutional support measures. The objective of the data collection is twofold: firstly, to identify ongoing challenges, and secondly, to propose practical strategies for individuals and organisations. These strategies include the optimisation of leadership models and the implementation of anti-harassment protocols.

This initiative signifies a continuous endeavour to harmonise the legal profession with international occupational health standards, as proposed by the International Bar Association (IBA). The synergy between studies such as 'Life in the Law' and the IBA's global principles reinforces the need for transnational approaches, capable of integrating local empirical evidence into universal guidelines. The 2025 edition incorporates distinct modules on the subjects of post-pandemic teleworking, flexible working hours and the impact of artificial intelligence on workload. These subjects represent emergent themes that necessitate adaptive responses from both individual professionals and regulatory bodies.

The integration of these research initiatives underscores

a pivotal paradigm: the viability of the legal profession is contingent upon the prioritisation of mental well-being as an inextricable element of ethics, efficiency and social justice.

The 'Life in the Law' study lends further support to the notion that lifestyles represent critical determinants of mental health and subjective, psychological and emotional well-being in the legal profession. Regular physical exercise, for instance, is recognised not only as a factor in promoting physical health, but above all as a mechanism for psychological benefit. This is in addition to strategies such as exposure to nature, a balanced diet, reading and mindfulness or meditation practices. When incorporated into the professional routine, these interventions act as stress moderators and cognitive resilience enhancers.

The study's conclusions indicate the necessity for a structural transformation in the organisational culture of the legal sector, driven by managers and leaders who have been trained to implement effective changes. In order to address this gap in the literature, it is recommended that specialised training in team management be prioritised, with an emphasis on psychosocial support skills. This training should be complemented by periodic assessments that guarantee methodological updating.

The promotion of well-being is regarded as a collective responsibility, necessitating the mobilisation of stakeholders across various sectors – encompassing professional bodies, academic institutions, and regulatory bodies – to establish sustainable work ecosystems.

The elimination of the stigma associated with mental health is of paramount importance, and should be facilitated through educational initiatives and awareness campaigns that seek to normalise discourse on the subject within the legal community. Concurrently, the study underscores the intersectional dimension of well-being, advocating for policies that take into account variables such as gender, ethnicity, disability, and sexual orientation when devising responses tailored to vulnerable groups.

Conducted during the peak of the pandemic (2020-2021), the study had already anticipated challenges and opportunities in the post-Covid-19 era. The pandemic has precipitated the adoption of hybrid working models, which offer greater flexibility and space for reflection on individual priorities. However, it has also exacerbated phenomena such as social isolation, work overload and the dissolution of boundaries between professional and personal life. This data underscores the duality of the pandemic's impact, demonstrating its role as both a catalyst for organisational innovation and an exacerbator of psychosocial risks.

The research concludes with a call for equal opportunities, arguing that individual potential can only be fully realised in an environment that values diversity, inclusion and mutual support. This vision is in alignment with the global principles of the International Bar Association (IBA), thereby reinforcing the necessity for synergies between local practices and international guidelines with a view to the establishment of a resilient and humanised legal profession.

Prosperity and Sustainability of Organisations - Report on the Cost of Stress and Psychological Health Problems at Work in Portugal

The fourth pertinent study in this analysis is the Report on the Cost of Stress and Psychological Health Problems at Work in Portugal (2023), published by the Portuguese Psychologists' Association (OPP).

This publicly available document discloses that the economic costs associated with work-related stress and psychological pathologies escalated by 62% between 2021 and 2023, reaching 5.3 billion euros – a figure commensurate with the national investment in pandemic mitigation measures in 2021. The report details that mental health-related absenteeism generated losses of 1.8 billion euros in 2022, while reduced productivity accounted for 5.3 billion, totalling an impact equivalent to 4% of Portugal's GDP.

At the European level, the phenomenon assumes macroeconomic proportions: the costs of absenteeism due to psychological reasons amount to 600 billion euros per annum, corresponding to 4% of the GDP of industrialised countries. The report also references data from the World Health Organisation (WHO, 2022), which estimates that 15% of the global working population will develop mental health problems, with aggregate costs of more than 1 trillion euros for the world economy.

In Portugal, 33 per cent of workers report experiencing conditions such as anxiety, depression or chronic stress, a figure that exceeds the European Union average.

Factors such as work intensity (which is characterised by 60% monotonous tasks, a figure that exceeds the European average) and dysfunctional organisational practices have been found to correlate with alarming rates. A survey of professionals revealed that 53% of respondents had experienced burnout, with 60% reporting daily physical exhaustion and 57% reporting mental exhaustion. According to the findings of epidemiological models that have been cited, occupational stress has been shown to increase the risk of acute myocardial infarction by 35% and mortality from cardiovascular pathologies by 17%.

The report advocates a proactive approach, in line with the OECD guidelines (2029), which call for the mandatory assessment of psychosocial risks and the integration of occupational psychologists into organisational strategies. For companies, the report makes the following recommendations:

1. The recruitment of psychologists with a specialism in the field of occupational health is underway.
2. The implementation of continuous monitoring systems for psychosocial risks is imperative.
3. The development of prevention plans founded upon empirical evidence.
4. The promotion of inclusive organisational cultures, accompanied by the implementation of anti-discrimination policies and the provision of self-care training, is of paramount importance.
5. The adoption of transformational leadership models, which prioritise well-being as a performance indicator, is of paramount importance.

The following recommendations are proposed by OPP

for consideration by relevant policymakers:

A revision of the legislation pertaining to occupational safety and health is required, with the objective of incorporating psychosocial criteria.

The allocation of specific funds for primary prevention programmes is imperative.

The integration of mental health indicators into the Single Report (Annexes C and D) is intended to standardise sectoral metrics. These recommendations underscore the necessity to transition from a reactive paradigm, characterised by a focus on treatment costs, to a preventive model. In this paradigm, psychological health is recognised as a strategic asset for business sustainability. The interplay between scientific evidence, public policies and organisational practices is identified as a critical factor in the mitigation of a crisis that, in addition to its human dimension, poses a threat to national economic competitiveness.

The Impact of Organisational Culture on the Mental Health and Well-Being of Legal Professionals

The fifth study, entitled 'The Impact of Organisational Culture on the Mental Health and Well-being of Legal Professionals' (November 2023), was carried out by ProChild CoLAB Against Poverty and Social Exclusion, the Psychology Research Centre of the University of Minho (CIPsi) and the Mental Law Association. This study took a pioneering look at psychosocial dynamics in the Portuguese legal sector.

The research, which was initiated under the assumption that legal professionals are confronted with elevated risks of developing psychological disorders due to the profession's inherently stressful nature, has substantiated a considerable prevalence of clinical symptoms: The results of the study indicated that 28 per cent of the participants exhibited symptoms of depression that were deemed to be clinically significant. Furthermore, 19 per cent of the participants displayed symptoms of anxiety, while 23 per cent exhibited critical levels of stress. These findings are in alignment with international data that points to a global crisis in the mental health of this professional class.

Methodologically, the study utilised an online assessment protocol comprising internationally validated questionnaires, including scales for depression (PHQ-9), anxiety (GAD-7), burnout (MBI-GS) and job satisfaction. Of the 868 respondents, 766 participants fully completed the protocol, with geographical representation concentrated in Lisbon (570 respondents). The demographic profile revealed a predominance of females (597 participants), a young age group (26-35 years: 336 cases) and an average of 13 years' professional experience in the field. A notable proportion of respondents, 35 per cent in fact, indicated their reluctance to pursue a career in the legal profession once more. This finding is widely regarded as a critical indicator of structural discontent.

In the diagnostic dimension, 286 participants (37.1%) reported a history of clinically validated psychological conditions, with depression and anxiety as the most frequent comorbidities. The analysis of adverse life events revealed that 301 professionals (38.9 per cent) had experienced traumatic events (such as bereavement or unemployment) in the last two years, an aggravating factor in psychosocial risk. Paradoxically, 779 respondents (95.3%) reported having a robust social support network, indicating that the existence of such networks does not inherently mitigate the impact of toxic work environments.

The reconciliation of professional obligations with familial commitments was identified as a pivotal challenge, with 54.7% of participants (n=423) reporting the absence of familial activities due to their professional commitments. The average score for this issue was 4.36 on a scale ranging from 1 (never) to 7 (always). In terms of financial circumstances, 58.1% (n=449) of respondents expressed the sentiment that 'personal finances control life', a notion that is concomitant with elevated levels of generalised anxiety ($r=0.42$, $p<0.01$).

These results serve to reinforce the hypothesis that

economic precariousness, which is associated with the culture of presentism in law firms (400 cases in Lisbon), functions as a transnational determinant of psychological malaise.

The study concluded that the intersection between archaic organisational practices (such as excessive face-to-face working hours: 390 cases), hierarchical pressures and the absence of work-life balance policies is fertile ground for emotional exhaustion.

The high prevalence of burnout (53 per cent with daily physical exhaustion) necessitates the urgent restructuring of management models, incorporating evidence that 65 per cent of professionals who would choose a legal career again do so conditional on the implementation of far-reaching reforms.

This evidence constitutes a vital contribution to the

design of evidence-based interventions and should guide the establishment of national occupational health observatories in the legal sector. The longitudinal replication of the study, with representative samples of independent professionals and judges, will allow for a deeper understanding of the regional and hierarchical asymmetries in this labour ecosystem that is critical for social justice.

The study identified critical patterns in the psychological health of this professional class, with urgent implications for sectoral policies. The study identified significant disparities associated with gender, age and labour context. Female participants demonstrated elevated levels of depressive symptoms (M=9.2, SD=6.1), anxiety (M=7.8, SD=5.4), and burnout (M=4.5, SD=1.2). This finding is notable in light of the absence of inter-gender differences in job satisfaction, suggesting a cultural normalisation of psychological distress among women in the sector.

The age variable emerged as a significant determining factor in the study. Professionals under the age of 35 exhibited a higher prevalence of mental disorders (35.7% with clinical symptoms of depression) and lower job satisfaction (M=2.8 on a scale of 1-7). This phenomenon was exacerbated by a shorter duration of professional experience ($r=-0.41$, $p<0.01$).

This evidence lends further support to the hypothesis that the initial phase of a legal career, characterised by hierarchical pressures and contractual instability, constitutes a period of heightened vulnerability.

The analysis of vital events revealed that 38.9% of participants exposed to negative events (bereavement, unemployment) developed clinical symptoms of anxiety (OR=2.3, 95%CI 1.8-2.9), underlining the interaction between occupational stress and external factors. However, the presence of robust social support was identified as a protective factor: professionals with a support network demonstrated a 54 per cent reduction in the risk of depression (RR=0.46, 95 per cent CI 0.38-0.55) and greater job satisfaction (M=5.1 vs. 2.9).

At the organisational level, structural differences were observed. Lawyers in law firms reported lower depressive symptoms (M=6.7 vs. 9.1 in individual practice) and higher job satisfaction (M=4.8 vs. 3.2). These differences may be associated with greater contractual stability and institutional resources. Conversely, self-employed professionals and trainees demonstrated critical levels of burnout (M=5.1, SD=1.4), reflecting the inherent precariousness of such practices.

Dissatisfaction with their professional choice emerged as a salient predictor, with the 35% who would not choose law again demonstrating a threefold risk of generalised anxiety (OR=3.1, 95%CI 2.4-4.0) and burnout levels 78% higher than the average. This correlation suggests that chronic psychological distress endangers not only individual well-being, but also the demographic sustainability of the profession.

It is concluded that the combination of individual factors (female gender, youth), contextual factors (lack of support, adverse events) and structural factors (job insecurity) calls for multi-level interventions. The microsphere requires leadership and mentoring programmes for young lawyers, as well as training in emotional resilience. In the macro-sphere, there is an urgent need to reformulate management models in law firms, implement gender balance quotas and regulate minimum conditions for independent practice.

As the authors observe, the transformation must be guided by an ethical paradox: professionals charged with defending social justice cannot remain victims of silent labour injustices.

Conclusions and recommendations

A comprehensive analysis of the extant literature on mental health in the legal profession reveals a multifaceted crisis with individual, organisational and socio-economic ramifications.

The International Bar Association (2023) report revealed that 35 per cent of legal professionals attribute direct negative impacts on their mental health to their work. This figure rises to 53 per cent in cases of burnout, according to data from the Portuguese Psychologists' Association (2023). This phenomenon is further compounded by intersectional disparities, as evidenced by the 'Life in the Law 2025' study. The study revealed that women, young people, ethnic minorities and disabled professionals exhibited a 42 per cent higher risk of developing depressive symptoms.

The combination of factors such as excessive workload (60% of tasks described as monotonous in Portugal), time pressure and toxic organisational cultures partially explains these results, but the root of the problem lies in the systemic normalisation of practices that are incompatible with human psychological functioning.

From an economic perspective, the direct and indirect costs of this crisis are exorbitant. In Portugal, for instance, productivity losses amounted to 5.3 billion euros in 2023, which is equivalent to the total investment in pandemic measures that occurred two years prior.

On a global scale, the World Health Organization (WHO) has estimated that mental health problems incur an annual cost of 1 trillion euros, with the legal sector contributing disproportionately due to its stress-inducing particularities. It is a matter of some irony that the investment in prevention has been demonstrated by OECD econometric models to be 13 times more profitable than remedying crises. This fact is, however, generally ignored by organisations, which instead prioritise short-term metrics over human sustainability.

The solution necessitates a comprehensive legislative and cultural re-engineering process. Firstly, it is imperative that the Bar Association implements concrete obligations. These obligations must include annual psychosocial risk assessments in all registered entities, minimum ratios of psychologists per employee (1:50), and the right to paid therapeutic leave.

Secondly, it is imperative that law firms discard outdated

management models that are based on invoiced hours. Instead, these firms should adopt productivity metrics that are in accordance with the European Work-Life Balance Directive (2024/789).

Thirdly, academic training in law should include compulsory subjects on emotional management and the ethics of self-care, as proposed by the Brazilian National Council of Justice since 2022.

The study 'Impact of Organisational Culture on Mental Health' (ProChild CoLAB, 2023) suggests that professionals in solo practice, despite facing increased risks of isolation, develop superior resilience strategies through autonomy in time management. It is suggested that traditional law firms can apply this lesson through non-punitive flexible working hours policies.

However, the attainment of independence does not

negate the necessity for formal support networks. The establishment of a National Legal Mental Health Observatory, as proposed in this paper, would facilitate the identification of specific vulnerabilities by region and speciality, thereby enabling the efficient targeting of resources.

The advent of the CoV-19 pandemic has precipitated a paradigm shift, with a significant proportion of professionals advocating for the permanent implementation of remote working. This data, when considered in conjunction with the evidence indicating a correlation between burnout cases and life-profession imbalances ($r=0.68$, $p<0.001$), serves to underscore the imperative for the implementation of public policies that regulate the right to digital disconnection within the legal sector. The British experience with the 'Legal Sector

Mental Health Charter' (2022), which reduced absenteeism by 22 per cent through the implementation of mandatory emotional check-ins, offers a replicable model.

The global mental health crisis currently being experienced by the legal profession has been thoroughly documented in a number of transnational studies. The report Mental Well-being in the Legal Profession (International Bar Association, 2023) identified that 35 per cent of lawyers attribute negative impacts of their work to their psychological well-being, a percentage that rises to 53 per cent in cases of burnout (Portuguese Psychologists' Association, 2023). This phenomenon is further compounded by intersectional disparities, as evidenced by the Life in the Law 2025 study. The study revealed that women, young people, ethnic minorities, and professionals with disabilities exhibited a 42 per cent higher risk of developing depressive symptoms. The combination of factors such as excessive workload (60% of tasks described as monotonous in Portugal), time pressure and toxic organisational cultures partially explains these results, but the root of the problem lies in the systemic normalisation of practices that are incompatible with human psychological functioning.

From an economic perspective, the direct and indirect costs of this crisis are exorbitant. In Portugal, for instance, productivity losses amounted to 5.3 billion euros in 2023, which is equivalent to the total investment in pandemic measures that occurred two years prior. On a global scale, the World Health Organization (WHO) has estimated that mental health problems incur an annual cost of 1 trillion euros, with the legal sector contributing disproportionately due to its stress-inducing particularities. It is a matter of some irony that the investment in prevention has been demonstrated by OECD econometric models to be 13 times more profitable than the resolution of crises. This fact is frequently ignored by organisations, which instead prioritise short-term metrics over human sustainability.

In summary, transformation necessitates concerted action across three domains: the individual (continuous training in socio-emotional skills), the organisational (management models grounded in neuroscientific evidence) and the systemic (legal frameworks that penalise psychosocial negligence).

The legal profession, the historical guardian of social justice, cannot continue to violate the principles it has sworn to uphold. Human dignity begins in the workplace.

As evidenced by the notable success stories from Scandinavia and Canada, where the implementation of these measures has led to a 40 per cent increase in talent retention, it can be concluded that mental well-being is not a cost, but rather the fundamental basis for an exceptional, ethical and sustainable legal profession.

Bibliography

ABA (2022). *National Lawyer Mental Health Survey.*

Abbott, A. (1988). *The System of Professions. University of Chicago Press.*

Acquah, A., Nsiah, T. K., Antie, E. N. A., & Otoo, B. (2021). *Literature review on theories of motivation.* EPRA *International Journal of Economic and Business Review, 9(5), 25-29.*

Ahmed, E. I. (2024). A systematic review of authentic leadership literature in educational research from 1997 to 2021. *Educational Management Administration & Leadership, 52(6),*

Aikman, D., Haldane, A. G., Hinterschweiger, M., & Kapadia, S. (2019). *Rethinking financial stability. Blanchard O.* e *Summers LH (a cura di), Evolution or Revolution, 16, 143-194.*

Aleksić, A. (2022). *Creating a Healthy Work Environment by Implementing Positive Organizational*

Behavior. Mathematical Statistician and Engineering Applications, 71(4),

AlShehhi, H., Alshurideh, M., Kurdi, B. A., & Salloum, S. A. (2020). *The impact of ethical leadership on employee's* A systematic review. *In International conference on advanced intelligent systems and informatics* 417-426). Cham: *Springer International Publishing.*

Alves, D. R. (2022). *Um olhar sobre o relatório do desenvolvimento humano*

Aryanti, R. D., Sari, E. Y. D., & Widiana, H. S. (2020, October). A literature review of workplace well-being. *In International Conference on Community Development (ICCD* (pp. 605-609). *Atlantis Press.*

Atkinson, C., Lupton, B., Kynighou, A., & Antcliff, V. (2022). *Small firms, owner managers and (strategic?) human resource management. Human Resource Management Journal, 32(2), 449-469.*

Austin, A., & Austin, A. (2020). *Theories of The foundations.* A universal declaration of human well-being, 15-24.

Avey, J. B., Luthans, F., Smith, R. M., & Palmer, N. F. (2010). *Impact of positive psychological capital on employee well-being over time. Journal of occupational health psychology, 15(1), 17.*

Bakker, A. B., & Demerouti, E. (2017). *Job demands–resources Taking stock and looking forward. Journal of occupational health psychology, 22(3), 273.*

Bauer, G. F., Hämmig, O., Cartwright, S., & Cooper, C. L. (2014). *Towards organizational* Stress, positive organizational behavior, and employee well-being. *Bridging occupational, organizational, and public* A transdisciplinary approach, 29-42.

Bezuidenhout, M. (2022). *Remuneration Strategies in the New Normal. In Managing Human The New Normal* 131-147). Cham: *Springer International Publishing.*

Bhende, P., Mekoth, N., Ingalhalli, V., & Reddy, Y. V. (2020). *Quality of work life and work–life balance. Journal of Human Values, 26(3), 256-265.*

Blustein, D. L., Lysova, E. I., & Duffy, R. D. (2023).

Understanding decent work and meaningful work. Annual Review of Organizational Psychology and Organizational Behavior, 10, 289-314.

Bolier, M., *Van der Lelij, A.* J., Janssens, G. O., van den Heuvel-Eibrink, M. M., & Neggers, S. J. (2023). Long-term safety of growth hormone replacement therapy in survivors of cancer and tumors of the pituitary region. Endocrine-related cancer, 30(7).

Borralho, L., de Jesus, S. N., Viseu, J., & Candeias, A. (2020). Avaliação da saúde dos professores portugueses: o Questionário de Saúde Docente. Psicologia, 34(1), 195-213.

Bronfenbrenner, U. (1979). *The Ecology of Human Development. Harvard University Press.*

Brough, P., Timms, C., Chan, X. W., Hawkes, A., & Rasmussen, L. (2020). Work–life balance: Definitions, causes, and consequences. *Handbook of socioeconomic determinants of occupational From macro-level to micro-level evidence, 473-487.*

Buchanan, B., Coyle, J., Brafford, A., Campbell, D.,

Camson, J., Gruber, C., & White, J. (2017). *The path to lawyer Practical recommendations for positive change (the report of the national task force on lawyer well-being), part II, recommendations for law schools.*

Buchanan, B., Coyle, J., Brafford, A., Campbell, D., Camson, J., Gruber, C., ... & White, J. (2017). *The path to lawyer Practical recommendations for positive change (the report of the national task force on lawyer well-being), part II, recommendations for law schools.*

Campbell, S. M. (2015). *The concept of well-being. In The Routledge handbook of philosophy of well-being* 402-414). Routledge.

Cannas, M., Sergi, B. S., Sironi, E., & Mentel, U. (2019). *Job satisfaction and subjective well-being in Europe. Economics & Sociology, 12(4), 183-196.*

Care, L. (2021). *Life in the Law*

Carr, A. (2013). *Positive The science of happiness and human strengths.* Routledge.

Cvenkel, N. (2021). Work-life balance and well-being at

work: Employees' perspective to promote a psychologically healthy workplace. *The Palgrave handbook of corporate social responsibility, 429-451.*

Daft, R. L. (2020). *Organization theory & design. Cengage learning.*

Danauskė, E., Raišienė, A. G., & Korsakienė, R. (2023). *Coping with burnout? Measuring the links between workplace conflicts, work-related stress, and burnout.* Business: *Theory and Practice, 24(1), 58-69.*

De Neve, J. E., & Ward, G. (2023). *Measuring workplace wellbeing.*

Delle Fave, A. (2020). *Eudaimonic and hedonic happiness. Encyclopedia of quality of life and well-being research, 1-7.*

Dervis, K., & Klugman, J. (2011). *Measuring human* the contribution of the *Human Development Index and related indices. Revue d'économie politique, 121(1), 73-92.*

Diener, E. (1984). *Subjective well-being. Psychological*

bulletin, 95(3), 542.

Diener, E. (2009). *The science of The collected works of Ed Diener* 37, pp. 11-58). *New* Springer.

Diener, E., & Biswas-Diener, R. (2019). Well-being interventions to improve societies. *Global Happiness Council, Global Happiness, and Well-being Policy Report, 95-110.*

Diener, E., Oishi, S., & Tay, L. (2018). *Advances in subjective well-being research. Nature human behaviour, 2(4), 253-260.*

Diener, E., Thapa, S., & Tay, L. (2020). *Positive emotions at work. Annual Review of Organizational Psychology and Organizational Behavior, 7, 451-477.*

Ding, H., & Yu, E. (2020). *Follower strengths-based leadership and follower innovative The roles of core self-evaluations and psychological well-being. Revista de Psicología del Trabajo y de las Organizaciones, 36(2), 103-110.*

Donaldson, S. I., Lee, J. Y., & Donaldson, S. I. (2019). *Evaluating positive psychology interventions at* A systematic review and meta-analysis. *International Journal of Applied Positive Psychology, 4, 113-134.*

Duncan, G. (2019). *Happiness and the new politicization of subjectivity. In Critical happiness studies* 83-97). Routledge.

D'Ambrosio, C., Jäntti, M., & Lepinteur, A. (2020). *Money and* Income, wealth, and subjective well-being. *Social Indicators Research, 148, 47-66.*

Egbekpalu, P. E. (2021). *Aristotelian concept of happiness (eudaimonia) and its conative role in human* A critical evaluation. *Conatus-Journal of Philosophy, 6(2), 75-86.*

Emmons, R. A., & Kaiser, H. A. (2014). *Goal orientation and emotional Linking goals and affect through the self. In Striving and feeling* 79-98). *Psychology Press.*

Eurofound Working Conditions in Europe Report.Kruger, A., & van der Merwe, H. (2021). *Journal of Occupational Health Psychology.*

Firouzbakht, M., & Tirgar, A. (2017). *Workplace social*

capital and employee a systematic review study. *Iranian Journal of Ergonomics, 5(1), 18-25.*

Fiske, S. T. (2022). *Ethical Empowerment in Legal Professions. Oxford University Press.*

Fredrickson, B. L. (2016). *The eudaimonics of positive emotions. Handbook of eudaimonic well-being, 183-190.*

Galani, A., & Galanakis, M. (2022). *Organizational Psychology on the Rise—McGregor's X and Y.* Theory: A. *Systematic Literature Review.* Psychology, 13(5), 782-789.

Gawel, J. E. (1996). Herzberg's theory of motivation and Maslow's hierarchy of needs. *Practical Assessment, Research, and Evaluation, 5(1), 11.*

Gragnano, A., Simbula, S., & Miglioretti, M. (2020). Work–life balance: weighing the importance of work–family and work–health balance. *International journal of environmental research and public health, 17(3), 907.*

Greipl, S., Klein, E., Lindstedt, A., Kiili, K., Moeller, K., Karnath, H. O., & Ninaus, M. (2021). *When the brain comes into Neurofunctional correlates of emotions and reward in game-based learning. Computers in Human Behavior, 125,*

Harley, B. (2015). *The one best way? 'Scientific 'research on HRM and the threat to critical scholarship. Human Resource Management Journal, 25(4), 399-407.*

Helliwell, J. (2001). *Social capital, the economy and well-being. The review of economic performance and social progress, 1.*

Helliwell, J. F., Huang, H., Norton, M., Goff, L., & Wang, S. (2023). *World happiness, trust and social connections in times of crisis. World happiness report.* (2023).

Hersey, P., & Blanchard, K. H. (1997). *Situational leadership. In Dean's Forum* 12, No. 2, p. 5).

Hesketh, I., & Cooper, C. (2023). *Wellbeing at* how to design, implement and evaluate an effective strategy. *Kogan Page Publishers.*

Hidalgo, J. L. T., Bravo, B. N., Martínez, I. P., Pretel, F. A., Postigo, J. M., & Rabadán, F. E. (2010).

Psychological well-being, assessment tools and related factors. Psychological well-being, 77-113.

Hill, E. J., & Carroll, S. J. (2021). Work-life harmony. *In Encyclopedia of quality of life and well-being research* 1-2). Cham: *Springer International Publishing.*

Ho, H., & Kuvaas, B. (2020). *Human resource management systems, employee well-being, and firm performance from the mutual gains and critical The well-being paradox. Human Resource Management, 59(3), 235-253.*

Hogan, S. J., & Coote, L. V. (2014). *Organizational culture, innovation, and* A test of Schein's model. *Journal of business research, 67(8),*

Huppert, F. A. (2009). A new approach to reducing disorder and improving well-being. *Perspectives on psychological science, 4(1), 108-111.*

Huppert, F. A. (2017). *Measurement really matters. Measuring wellbeing series; discussion paper, 2.*

Huppert, F. A., & So, T. T. (2013). *Flourishing across Application of a new conceptual framework for defining well-being. Social indicators research, 110, 837-861.*

Huta, V. (2016). *An overview of hedonic and eudaimonic well-being concepts. The Routledge handbook of media use and well-being, 14-33.*

International Bar Association. (2021). *Mental wellbeing in the legal* A global study. London: *International Bar Association.*

Jago, A. G. (1982). Leadership: *Perspectives in theory and research. Management science, 28(3), 315-336.*

Jesuíno, J. (1999). *Processos de Liderança. Livros Horizonte, Lisboa.* ISBN 972-24-0990-1.

Kahneman, D., Diener, E., & Schwarz, N. (Eds.). (1999). Well-being: *Foundations of hedonic psychology. Russell Sage Foundation.*

Kellerman, B. (2024). *Bad leadership-Why we steer clear.* Leadership, 20(6), 402-410.

Kelliher, C., Richardson, J., & Boiarintseva, G. (2019). *All of work? All of life? Reconceptualising work-life balance for the 21st century. Human resource management journal, 29(2), 97-112.*

Keyes, C. L. (2002). *The mental health From languishing to flourishing in life. Journal of health and social behavior, 207-222.*

Keyes, C.L.M. (2005). *Mental illness and/or mental health? American Psychologist.*

Khindri, A., & Tanwar, S. (2023). Trait-competitiveness and life-satisfaction: A moderated mediation model of hard-work and leisure. *Personality and Individual Differences, 200,*

Kim, M., Kim, A. C. H., Newman, J. I., Ferris, G. R., & Perrewé, P. L. (2019). *The antecedents and consequences of positive organizational The role of psychological capital for promoting employee well-being in sport organizations. Sport Management Review, 22(1), 108-125.*

Klugman, J. (2009). *Human development report Overcoming Human mobility and development. Overcoming Human Mobility and Development (October 5,* UNDP-HDRO *Human Development Reports.*

Kopp, M. S., Stauder, A., Purebl, G., Janszky, I., &

Skrabski, A. (2008). *Work stress and mental health in a changing society. European Journal of Public Health, 18(3), 238-244.*

Krill, P. R., Johnson, R., & Albert, L. (2016). *The prevalence of substance use and other mental health concerns among American attorneys. Journal of Addiction Medicine, 10(1), 46-52.*

Krill, P. R., Johnson, R., & Albert, L. (2016). *The prevalence of substance use and other mental health concerns among American attorneys. Journal of Addiction Medicine, 10(1), 46.*

Kumar, S., Sarkar, S., & Chahar, B. (2023). A systematic review of work-life integration and role of flexible work arrangements. *International Journal of Organizational Analysis, 31(3), 710-736.*

Kun, A., & Gadanecz, P. (2019). *Workplace happiness, well-being, and their relationship with psychological* A study of *Hungarian Teachers. Current Psychology, 1-15.*

Ladkin, D., & Patrick, C. B. (2022). *Whiteness in leadership* A critical analysis of race in Bass' transformational leadership theory. Leadership, 18(2), 205-223.

Larsen, R. J., & Eid, M. (2008). *Ed Diener and the science of subjective well-being. The science of subjective well-being, 1-13.*

Latham, G. P., & Budworth, M. H. (2020). *The study of work motivation in the 20th and 21st centuries. Historical Perspectives in Industrial and Organizational Psychology, 203-226.*

Le Nguyen, K. D., & Fredrickson, B. L. (2017). *Positive emotions and well-being. Positive Established and emerging issues, 29-45.*

Leithwood, K., & Louis, K. S. (Eds.). (2021). *Organizational learning in schools. Taylor & Francis.*

Locke, E. A., & Latham, G. P. (2019). *The development of goal setting* A half century retrospective. *Motivation Science, 5(2), 93.*

Lopez, S. J., & Snyder, C. R. (Eds.). (2009). *The Oxford handbook of positive psychology. Oxford University Press.*

Madison, J., Hamilton, A., Franklin, B., Washington, G., Claire, E., & TESOL, M. (2021). *The Constitution of the United States. Independently Published.*

Mahmoud, R., Al-Mkhadmeh, A. A., & Alananzeh, O. A. (2021). *Exploring the relationship between human resources management practices in the hospitality sector and service innovation in* the mediating role of human capital. *Geo Journal of Tourism and Geosites, 35(2), 507-514.*

Malik, K. (2013). *Human development report The rise of the Human progress in a diverse world. The Rise of the Human Progress in a Diverse World (March 15,* UNDP-HDRO *Human Development Reports.*

Maslow, A. H. (1998). *Maslow on management. John Wiley & Sons.*

Mather, L. (2003). *What do clients want-What do Lawyers do. Emory LJ, 52.* (1065).

McArthur, J. (2023). *Rethinking authentic* work, well-being, and society. *Higher education, 85(1), 85-101.*

McDonough, P. (2000). *Job insecurity and health. International journal of health services, 30(3), 453-*

476.

Navy, S. L. (2020). *Theory of human motivation—Abraham Maslow. Science Education in Theory and An Introductory Guide to Learning Theory, 17-28.*

Nikolova, M., & Cnossen, F. (2020). *What makes work meaningful and why economists should care about it. Labour economics, 65,*

Oades, L. G., & Dulagil, A. (2016). *Workplace and organizational well-being. The wiley blackwell handbook of the psychology of positivity and strengths-based approaches at work, 248-271.*

Obrenovic, B., Jianguo, D., Khudaykulov, A., & Khan, M. A. S. (2020). Work-family conflict impact on psychological safety and psychological well-being: A job performance model. *Frontiers in psychology, 11, 475.*

OECD (2022). *Mental Health and* Impact, *Challenges and Policy Responses.*

OMS (2013). *Plano de Ação para a Saúde Mental*

OMS. (2016). *Mental health in the workplace.*

Pardee, R. L. (1990). *Motivation Theories of Maslow, Herzberg, McGregor & McClelland.* A. *Literature Review of Selected Theories Dealing with Job Satisfaction and Motivation.*

Park, J. (2022). *The Effect of Leadership on Job Satisfaction and Organizational Commitment-Focused on genuine leadership. Journal of Digital Convergence, 20(2), 155-161.*

Paulus, P. (2023). *The Effect of Remuneration, Work Discipline and Motivation on Employee Performance. Golden Ratio of Human Resource Management, 3(1), 23-32.*

Payne, M. (2020). *Modern social work theory. Bloomsbury Publishing.*

Peccei, R., & *Van De Voorde, K.* (2019). *Human resource management-well-being-performance research* Past, present, and future. *Human resource management journal, 29(4), 539-563.*

Peiró, J. M., Bayona, J. A., Caballer, A., & *Di Fabio, A.* (2020). *Importance of work characteristics affects job The mediating role of individual dispositions on the work design-performance relationships. Personality and Individual Differences, 157,*

Perlow, L. (2020). *Finding How corporations, individuals, and families can benefit from new work practices. Cornell University Press.*

Perrin, T., May, H., & Milwain, E. (2008). *Wellbeing in An occupational approach for therapists and carers. Elsevier Health Sciences.*

Pessoa, F. (1982). *Livro do* II. Atica.

Pondy, L. R., & Mitroff, I. I. (1979). *Beyond open system models of organization. Research in organizational behavior, 1(1), 3-39.*

Pradhan, R. K., & Hati, L. (2022). *The measurement of employee* development and validation of a scale. *Global Business Review, 23(2), 385-407.*

Prilleltensky, I., & Prilleltensky, O. (2021). *How people Why it affects health, happiness, love, work, and society. Cambridge University Press.*

Robertson, I. T., Cooper, C. L., & Johnson, S. (2011). Well-being: *Productivity and happiness at work* 3). Basingstoke: *Palgrave Macmillan.*

Rodríguez-Muñoz, A., & Sanz-Vergel, A. I. (2013). *Happiness and well-being at* A special issue introduction. *Revista de Psicología del Trabajo y de las Organizaciones, 29(3), 95-97.*

Ryan, J. (2007). *Inclusive* A review. *Journal of Educational Administration and Foundations, 18(1-2), 92-125.*

Ryan, R. M., & Deci, E. L. (2017). Self-determination theory: *Basic psychological needs in motivation, development, and wellness. Guilford publications.*

Ryff, C. D. (2013). *Psychological well-being Advances in the science and practice of eudaimonia. Psychotherapy and psychosomatics, 83(1), 10-28.*

Ryff, C. D., & Singer, B. H. (2008). *Know thyself and become what you* A eudaimonic approach to psychological well-being. *Journal of happiness studies, 9, 13-39.*

Ryff, C. D., Boylan, J. M., & Kirsch, J. A. (2021). *Advancing the science of well-being. Measuring Well-Being.*

Salas-Vallina, A., & Alegre, J. (2021). *Happiness at Developing a shorter measure. Journal of Management & Organization, 27(3), 460-480.*

Schulte, P. A., Sauter, S. L., Pandalai, S. P., Tiesman, H. M., Chosewood, L. C., Cunningham, T. R., ... & Howard, J. (2024). *An urgent call to address work-related psychosocial hazards and improve worker well-being. American journal of industrial medicine, 67(6), 499-514.*

Schulte, P., & Vainio, H. (2010). Well-being at work–overview and perspective. *Scandinavian journal of work, environment & health, 422-429.*

Schultz, D. P., & Schultz, S. E. (2020). *Psychology and work today.* Routledge.

Seaborn, K., Pennefather, P., & Fels, D. I. (2020). *Eudaimonia and hedonia in the design and evaluation of a cooperative game for psychosocial well-being.* Human–Computer Interaction, 35(4), 289-337.

Seligman, M. E. (2019). *Positive* A personal history. *Annual review of clinical psychology, 15, 1-23.*

Seligman, M. E., & Csikszentmihalyi, M. (2000). *Positive An introduction* 55, No. 1, p. 5). *American Psychological Association.*

Seligman, M.E.P. (2011). Flourish: A. *Visionary New Understanding of Happiness and Well-being. Free Press.*

Sfeatcu, R., Cernuşcă-Miţariu, M., Ionescu, C., Roman, M., Cernuşcă-Miţariu, S., Coldea, L., ... & Burcea, C. C. (2014). *The concept of wellbeing in relation to health and quality of life. European Journal of Science and Theology, 10(4), 123-128.*

Steers, R. M., Mowday, R. T., & Shapiro, D. L. (2004). *The future of work motivation theory. Academy of Management review, 29(3), 379-387.*

Steffgen, G., Sischka, P. E., & *Fernandez de Henestrosa, M.* (2020). *The quality of work index and the quality of employment* A multidimensional approach of job quality and its links to well-being at work. *International Journal of Environmental Research and Public Health, 17(21).* (7771).

Stevenson, D. (2017). *Thriving at The Stevenson/Farmer review of mental health and employers.* London: *Department for Work and Pensions and Department of Health.*

Stogdill, R. M. (1975, August). *The Evolution of Leadership Theory. In Academy of Management Proceedings* 1975, No. 1, pp. 4-6). *Briarcliff Manor, NY Academy of Management.*

Stouten, J., Rousseau, D. M., & *De Cremer, D.* (2018). *Successful organizational Integrating the management practice and scholarly literatures. Academy of Management Annals, 12(2), 752-788.*

Suh, E. M., & Oishi, S. (2002). *Subjective well-being across cultures. Online readings in psychology and culture, 10(1), 1.*

Susskind, R. (2023). Tomorrow's lawyers: *An introduction to your future. Oxford University Press.*

Taormina, R. J., & Gao, J. H. (2013). *Maslow and the motivation Measuring satisfaction of the needs. The American journal of psychology, 126(2), 155-177.*

Tausig, M. (2013). *The sociology of work and well-being. Handbook of the sociology of mental health, 433-455.*

Thilagavathy, S., & Geetha, S. N. (2021). Work-life balance-a systematic review. Vilakshan-XIMB *Journal of Management, 20(2), 258-276.*

Tudor, K. (2017). *Mental health stigma and the legal profession. International Journal of Law and Psychiatry.*

Tzima, S., & Slaby, J. (2024). *Political philosophy of* inverting the concepts, expanding the niche. *Phenomenology and the Cognitive Sciences, 1-24.*

Usher, A., & Kober, N. (2012). 1. *What Is Motivation and Why Does It Matter? Center on Education Policy.*

Voordt, T. V. D., & Jensen, P. A. (2023). *The impact of healthy workplaces on employee satisfaction, productivity, and costs. Journal of Corporate Real Estate, 25(1), 29-49.*

Vroom, V., Porter, L., & Lawler, E. (2015). *Expectancy theories. In Organizational Behavior 1* 94-113). Routledge.

Warr, P. (2020). 32 *Happiness in Its Many Forms. The Cambridge Handbook of Workplace Affect, 426.*

Warr, P., & Nielsen, K. (2018). *Wellbeing and work*

performance. Handbook of well-being. Salt Lake City, DEF Publishers.

Weziak-Bialowolska, D., Bialowolski, P., Sacco, P. L., VanderWeele, T. J., & McNeely, E. (2020). Well-being in life and well-being at work: *Which comes first? Evidence from a longitudinal study. Frontiers in Public Health, 8, 103.*

World Health Organization. (2021). *Investing in our* a comprehensive agenda for the health and well-being of children and adolescents.

World Health Organization. (2022). *World mental health Transforming mental health for all. World Health Organization.*

Zapf, D., Kern, M., Tschan, F., Holman, D., & Semmer, N. K. (2021). *Emotion* A work psychology perspective. *Annual Review of Organizational Psychology and Organizational Behavior, 8, 139-172.*

Zou, L. (2023). *The Many Facets of Exploring Fiedler's Contingency Theory. Perspectives in Social Sciences and Arts, 1(1), 1-5.*

Author's biographical note Fernando Messias

Fernando Messias was born in Lisbon, Portugal.

The individual in question possesses a Juris Doctor (J.D.) degree, in addition to being a practising lawyer, arbitrator, mediator and legal consultant. His academic credentials include a Postgraduate Diploma in International Arbitration (PGDip), a Master's in International Trade Law (LL.M), a Ph.D. in Tourism, and a Post-Doctorate in Psychology.

As a practising lawyer, he has gained experience in both domestic and international contexts. He has specialised in advocating for ethical principles and has been instrumental in promoting a creative, innovative and responsible approach to legal practice. Utilising his proficiency as an arbitrator, mediator, and holder of advanced qualifications in International Arbitration and International Trade Law, he has engaged in domestic and international arbitrations, thereby promoting cross-border trade and alternative dispute resolution.

In his capacity as a legal consultant, the subject has acquired a specialism in real estate, tourism, industry, investment and business law, with a focus on the facilitation of secure and efficient legal operations for a client base. His research as a doctoral and post-doctoral scholar focuses on law, arbitration, international trade, organisational psychology, hospitality, management, human resources, leadership, and workplace well-being. He collaborates with entrepreneurs and companies to enhance performance and drive organisational success.

Fernando is also a published author, with works

spanning the genres of science fiction, knowledge dissemination and visual art. Furthermore, he possesses multiple postgraduate qualifications and is a certified facilitator in creative problem-solving using the Basadur Simplex Method.

Foreword's Biographical Note Raquel Sampaio

Raquel Sampaio is a legal professional with over two decades of experience, whose career has proven to be fruitful, with diverse international experience in countries such as East Timor, New York, and Mozambique. She currently works as a consultant in the Public Law Department at SRS Legal, a law firm.

Her career now extends beyond the legal field, encompassing mental health as a strategic priority in professional contexts through her role as executive director of the Associação Direito Mental (Mental Health Association) and Mind Alliance Portugal. In this context, Raquel Sampaio challenges established conventions by integrating mental health as a strategic pillar in professional spaces.

Foreword's Biographical Note Saúl Neves de Jesus

Saúl Neves de Jesus is a Full Professor of Psychology, having previously served as Vice-Rector of the University of Algarve from 2017 to 2021.

He is Director of the Doctoral Course in Psychology, Coordinator of the University Centre for Research in Psychology (CUIP), and is also Portugal's representative on the 'Stress, Trauma, Anxiety and Resilience Society' (STAR).

He has held the positions of President of the Board of Directors, President of the Scientific Council and President of the Pedagogical Council of the Faculty of Humanities and Social Sciences. Furthermore, he fulfilled the role of Coordinator of the National Psychology Forum from 2020 to 2025.

He has provided supervision to the post-doctoral studies of colleagues from a range of international backgrounds and has overseen the completion of 53 doctoral theses.

He has published extensively, with more than three hundred scientific articles appearing in peer-reviewed international journals.

Publications

Law & Business

Messias, F. (2013). Company Law Analysis and Leadership in Risk Taking – The Portuguese Company Scenario (English edition). Allahabad, India: Rochak Publishing.

Messias, F. (2013). Corporate Governance and Corporate Lawyers – Company Laws in Portugal and Risk Analysis(English edition). Allahabad, India: Rochak Publishing.

Messias, F. (2013). Corporate Social Responsibility – Is Your Company in Portugal on the Right Track? (English edition). Allahabad, India: Rochak Publishing.

Messias, F. (2013). Novas perspectivas na responsabilidade do Estado – O impacto da liderança organizacional no bem-estar dos trabalhadores (Portuguese edition). Allahabad, India: Rochak Publishing.

Messias, F. (2014). Nouvelles perspectives dans la responsabilité de l'Etat – L'impact du leadership organisationnel sur le bien-être des employés (French edition). Allahabad, India: Rochak Publishing.

Messias, F. (2013). Portugal – Analysis of the Company Laws and Corporate Social Responsibility: Does Leadership and Employee Well-Being Matter? (English edition). Allahabad, India: Rochak Publishing.

Messias, F. (2013). Leadership & Management Litigation Risk – A Mental Model Methodology to Reduce the Risk of Claims for Damage to the Company Following "Bad" Business Decisions: The Portuguese Company Scenario (English edition). Allahabad, India: Rochak Publishing.

Messias, F. (2015). O Bem-Estar Organizacional na Hotelaria de Cinco Estrelas: O papel da Liderança Promotora de Bem-Estar (Portuguese edition). Allahabad, India: Rochak Publishing.

Messias, F. (2015). The Organizational Well-Being in Five-Star Hospitality: The Role of Leadership Which Promotes Well-Being (English edition). Allahabad, India: Rochak Publishing.

Messias, F. (2015). Bien-être organisationnel dans l'Hôtellerie Cinq étoiles: Le rôle du leadership promoteur de bien-être(French edition). Allahabad, India: Rochak Publishing.

Messias, F. (2015). Liderança e bem-estar: o caso da hotelaria de cinco estrelas no Algarve (Doctoral thesis, 1st edition). Santo Tirso, Portugal: Editorial Novembro.

Messias, F. (2017). Liderança e bem-estar: o caso da hotelaria de cinco estrelas no Algarve (Doctoral thesis,

2nd edition). Santo Tirso, Portugal: Editorial Novembro.

Messias, F. (2018). The Organizational Well-Being in Five-Star Hospitality: The Role of Leadership Which Promotes Well-Being (2nd ed., English edition). Allahabad, India: Rochak Publishing.

Messias, F. (2018). Can, and if so in what circumstances would, the United Nations Convention on Contracts for the International Sale of Goods be the proper law governing an arbitration agreement? (English first edition). Allahabad, India: Rochak Publishing.

Messias, F. (2018). International Arbitration: Multi-party Arbitration and the Arbitrator's Duty of Disclosure (English edition). Allahabad, India: Rochak Publishing.

Messias, F. (2019). The Impact of Technological Innovations on International Trade and Finance: The Importance of E-commerce and the Documentary Credit

Particularly on Export Financing (English edition). Allahabad, India: Rochak Publishing.

Messias, F. (2019). A Critical Reflection on the Relationship Between WTO Law, Intellectual Property Law, and Investment Law: The Particular Issue of Compulsory Licensing of Medicines (English edition). Allahabad, India: Rochak Publishing.

Messias, F. (2019). Bem-estar: conceitos e teorias de bem-estar e fatores influenciadores do bem-estar no trabalho(Portuguese edition). Allahabad, India: Rochak Publishing.

Messias, F. (2020). Liderança organizacional: conceitos e principais teorias (Portuguese edition). Allahabad, India: Rochak Publishing.

Messias, F. (2020). A cor e a palavra: criatividade e subjetividade de estilos em arte visual. Santo Tirso, Portugal: Editorial Novembro.

Messias, F. (2020). Modelos e perspetivas de bem-estar organizacional (Portuguese edition). Allahabad, India: Rochak Publishing.

Messias, F. (2020). Liderança nas organizações: a liderança promotora de bem-estar (Portuguese edition). Allahabad, India: Rochak Publishing.

Messias, F. (2022). A importância da liderança promotora de bem-estar na hotelaria de cinco estrelas: uma revisão sistemática da literatura (Portuguese edition). Allahabad, India: Rochak Publishing.

Messias, F. (2024). O Rei e a Rainha – A família Arehns. Santo Tirso, Portugal: Editorial Novembro.

Messias, F. (2024). Direito, Poder Paternal, Ciberespaço e Violência Escolar: do mundo virtual ao papel dos pais como líderes promotores de bem-estar (Portuguese edition). Allahabad, India: Rochak Publishing.

Messias, F. (2025). Advocacia e Bem-Estar (Portuguese edition). Allahabad, India: Rochak Publishing.

Messias, F. (2025). A prática do Direito e da Arbitragem Internacional na Era da Inteligência Artificial (Portuguese edition). Allahabad, India: Rochak Publishing.

Messias, F. (2025). Can, and if so in what circumstances would, the United Nations Convention on Contracts for the International Sale of Goods be the proper law governing an arbitration agreement? (English second edition). Allahabad, India: Rochak Publishing.

Chapters

Law & Business

Messias, F. (2011). Portugal – Analysis of the Company Laws. In W. H. Byrnes (Ed.), International Trust Laws and Analysis: Company Laws, Wealth Management & Tax Planning Strategies. Kluwer Law International.

Messias, F. (2017). Portugal – Analysis of the Company Laws. In W. H. Byrnes (Ed.), International Trust Laws and Analysis: Company Laws, Wealth Management & Tax Planning Strategies. Kluwer Law International.

Messias, F. (2020). Portugal – Analysis of the Company Laws. In W. H. Byrnes (Ed.), International Trust Laws and Analysis: Company Laws, Wealth Management & Tax Planning Strategies. Kluwer Law International.

Fiction & Essay

Heine, E. (2014). A Passagem (Portuguese edition). Allahabad, India: Cyberwit.net.

Heine, E. (2014). Le Passage (French edition). Allahabad, India: Cyberwit.net.

Heine, E. (2015). O Ventre e o Medo (Portuguese edition). Allahabad, India: Cyberwit.net.

Heine, E. (2016). Le ventre et la peur (French edition). Allahabad, India: Cyberwit.net.

Johakin, S. (2014). Dois Sonhos (Portuguese edition). Allahabad, India: Cyberwit.net.

Johakin, S. (2014). Deux rêves (French edition). Allahabad, India: Cyberwit.net.

Johakin, S. (2016). O Olhar de Deus (Portuguese edition). Allahabad, India: Cyberwit.net.

Johakin, S. (2016). Le Regard de Dieu (French edition). Allahabad, India: Cyberwit.net.

Messias, F. (2013). A Verdade Oculta da Descoberta da América: Poemário Filosófico a Cristóvão Colon (Bilingual English and Portuguese edition). Allahabad, India: Cyberwit.net.

Messias, F. (2014). La Vérité Cachée de la Découverte de l'Amérique: Ensemble de Poèmes Philosophiques à Christophe Colomb (Bilingual French and Portuguese edition). Allahabad, India: Cyberwit.net.

Messias, F., & Liba, M. (2012). Narrar em Português – Poemas Selecionados (Portuguese edition). Allahabad, India: Cyberwit.net.

Sabóia, A. (2015). Abandonment (English edition). Allahabad, India: Cyberwit.net.

Sabóia, A. (2015). A Borboleta (Portuguese edition). Allahabad, India: Cyberwit.net.

Stolkin, E. (2015). O Rei e a Rainha – O Palácio Arehns (Portuguese edition). Allahabad, India: Cyberwit.net.

Stolkin, E. (2015). Le Roi et la Reine – Le Palais Arehns (French edition). Allahabad, India: Cyberwit.net.

Articles

Messias, F., Mendes, J., & Monteiro, I. (2010). The effects of leadership behaviors on employee well-being in the workplace: A worthy investment from managers or leaders. In Proceedings of the 6th International Symposium on Entrepreneurship in Tourism (pp. 141–159). Universidade do Algarve, Faro, Portugal.

Messias, F., Mendes, J., & Monteiro, I. (2011). Liderança e bem-estar na hotelaria no Algarve. First International Conference on Tourism and Management Studies, ESGHT, Universidade do Algarve.

Messias, F., Mendes, J., & Monteiro, I. (2011). Leadership and wellbeing in hospitality industry, new challenges. Conference on Modern Hospitality and Tourism Development, Allmed University, Tehran, Iran.

Messias, F. (2016). Comportamentos do líder promotor de bem-estar na hotelaria de cinco estrelas. Proceedings of the International Congress on Interdisciplinary in Social and Human Sciences, Universidade do Algarve.

Messias, F. B. (2016). A importância da liderança na hotelaria de cinco estrelas. Publituris, (1314), 30.

Messias, F. (2024). A parentalidade e a regulação das responsabilidades parentais: Os pais no papel de líderes promotores de bem-estar. In F. Bayle (Ed.), Perturbações da Parentalidade II. Editorial Novembro.

Messias, F. (2025). Dispute Resolution and Prevention: Europe, Morocco, and Saudi Arabia - Venues for the 2030 and 2034 FIFA World Cup. Paper presented at the seminar Dispute Resolution and Prevention, ICAM, Madrid.

Messias, F. (2025). International Arbitration in the Age of Artificial Intelligence. In R. L. Lobo (Ed.), White Book

Developments on International Arbitration 2025: Future is Now. IIMAT.

Participation in Academic Examination Boards

Doctoral thesis jury

Member of the jury for the thesis 'Satisfaction of hotel professionals: study of the relationships with personal and organisational variables' by Sérgio Jorge Pereira Da Borralha, as part of a PhD in Psychology at the Faculty of Psychology, University of Algarve (2018).

Master's dissertation jury

Member of the jury for the thesis 'Geoeconomics of the Portuguese Continental Shelf: Cruise Tourism' by José Gregório Gustavo Rodriguez Gonçalves, as part of the Master's Degree in Land Management – Remote Sensing and Geographic Information Systems, at the Faculty of Social and Human Sciences of the New University of Lisbon (2019).

www.ingramcontent.com/pod-product-compliance
Lightning Source LLC
LaVergne TN
LVHW100138061126
851857LV00010B/141